IN A BESIEGED CITY

International Testimonies of the Lord's Love

Compiled and Edited by Cheryl Johnson Barton

Warner Press
Anderson, Indiana

Coordinator of Publishing & Creative Services
Church of God Ministries, Inc.
PO Box 2420
Anderson, IN 46018-2420
800-848-2464 • www.chog.org

To purchase additional copies of this book, to inquire about distribution, and for all other sales-related matters, please contact:

Warner Press, Inc.
PO Box 2499
Anderson, IN 46018-2499
800-741-7721 • www.warnerpress.org

Cover photo by Cheryl Johnson Barton.
Cover and text design by Mary Jaracz.
Edited by Stephen R. Lewis.

ISBN-13: 978-159317-510-8

Printed in the United States of America.
10 11 12 13 14 15 16 /EP/ 10 9 8 7 6 5 4 3 2 1

Table of Contents

Introduction

Book and story titles are very important. I have prayed over each of the titles, including ***In a Besieged City***, that have adorned the covers of the fifteen books in this series of international testimonies I've compiled and edited since 1993. I am well aware that unless the title compels the reader, the book is not likely to be read.

Which is why I was so surprised to be led to this year's title. I would have preferred a more positive, genuinely inviting title to put a smile on the face. But I kept being drawn back to Psalm 31 and especially to "in a besieged city," four words in verse 21. Shrugging my shoulders in wonderment, I titled this book.

Little did I know that less than a month later I would be diagnosed with renal cell carcinoma. Although my diseased kidney was surgically removed in Japan in early April and I made a swift recovery, the cancer returned in September. Doctors in Japan and the United States agreed that cancer will besiege me for the rest of my life. "Sit Still, My Daughter," one of the stories in this book, recounts God's comforting presence when the recurrence was diagnosed.

In October came the news that cancer was again stalking my friend whose triumphant story "Whether I Live or Die" had been published only four months earlier in last year's testimony book, *River of Delights*. (Her photograph from Laos also graces that book's cover.) How could this cancer have returned when only in May she'd been released by doctors to resume her overseas assignment? The whole missionary community and the worldwide church mourned Susan's death on January 7, 2010. Her siege was over, but questions that remained and lacked satisfying answers could not be denied.

Illness isn't the only siege that threatens us. In this book you'll read about three natural calamities, in "Disaster in the Philippines" (typhoon), "And God Is in It" (earthquake), and "The Fingerprints of God" (mudslides). You'll also learn about other sieges of different kinds that so easily sap our energy and sense of well-being: civil war in Colombia ("In a

Besieged City"), severe birth defects in New Zealand ("A Miracle Named Rhea"), schedules ("In the Palm of His Hand"), and confusing doubt ("Wading with God").

We experience sieges more often than we'd like. They just seem to come with life on this imperfect earth—the reason Christians look ahead expectantly to heaven where, "He will wipe every tear from their eyes. There will be no more death or mourning or crying or pain, for the old order of things has passed away" (Revelation 21:4).

If we remember only the words ***In a Besieged City***, we will indeed be trapped there. But there is unbounded hope in the psalmist's declaration: "Praise be to the LORD, for he showed his wonderful love to me when I was ***In a Besieged City***. In my alarm I said, 'I am cut off from your sight!' Yet you heard my cry for mercy when I called to you for help" (Psalm 31:21–22).

The testimonies in this book ring out, "Amen and amen!" Be encouraged as you read them and remember God's love for you in your own besieged city. Then please give a copy of this book to someone imprisoned by siege and searching for freedom. Sieges cannot last forever, for only God is eternal. Rejoice with me and praise his name!

—Cheryl Johnson Barton, editor

FOR THE SIEGE

"This is what the LORD says to you: 'Do not be afraid or discouraged because of this vast army. For the battle is not yours, but God's…You will not have to fight this battle. Take up your positions; stand firm and see the deliverance the LORD will give you…Do not be afraid; do not be discouraged. Go out and face them tomorrow, and the LORD will be with you.'" —2 Chronicles 20:15, 17

"...in all these things we are more than conquerors through him who loved us." —Romans 8:37

Her parents banished her; God welcomed her.

The Prodigal Daughter

by Kay Critser
(Yamoussoukro, Côte d'Ivoire)

We had just stepped down from the mission vehicle to spread out in groups across Belleville, a small subdivision of Bobo-Dioulasso in Burkina Faso, Côte d'Ivoire's neighbor to the north. Our purpose was to share the tract "Help from Above" with those to whom the Spirit of God would lead us. We had a translation in French and one in Dioula, the trade language of many of the ethnic groups of this new land to which God was calling us.

Anne Yeo, a Dioula speaker and pastor's wife, and I approached a small enclosure of woven grass alongside a main dirt road of the residential area. There we found a beautiful young woman sitting behind a makeshift table on which some packets of hair mesh and a few jars of hair cream were waiting to be purchased. As we greeted her, she welcomed us to sit. Upon introducing ourselves, we learned that her name was Adeline. She was a self-made beautician, mostly braiding hair since she had no other amenities found in an established salon.

We were quickly interrupted by a little boy rushing into the narrow enclosure and straight into Adeline's arms. He turned to look at us, curious about the strangers who'd appeared suddenly. However, he did not stay long since his little friends—just as curious—were waiting on him.

Anne began to explain our purpose for dropping by Adeline's roadside business. The young mother remarked that she'd grown up in a Christian home in the village and had been a Christian. But when she got pregnant, her parents chased her away. She decided to follow the man whose baby she carried. To her dismay, he was a Muslim and refused to allow her to attend church.

As we talked, Adeline's three-year-old son scurried into the grass shelter to grab a handful of cooked rice from a covered plate that had been tucked

Kay Critser and Pastor Emmanuel Yao handing out tracts at a roadside stand

away since perhaps lunch. From the plate's appearance, it wasn't his first time there. We inquired about his name. "Mohammed," she answered.

Once again my colleague Anne turned our thoughts back to the point of our visit—to help Adeline understand that God loved her even now. I shared the Bible story of the son who'd made a bad decision and left home. Even when the prodigal was still far off, his father was waiting for his return with open arms and forgiveness. The son's guilt was erased, and the story ends with rejoicing.

Though Adeline's story is not exactly the same, she admitted she knew she'd done wrong. Anne and I assured her that God was not angry as she might have thought these last three years because of her Christian parents' rejection. But Jesus was saddened because she did not understand that her guilt could be exchanged for forgiveness. After we asked her to read 1 John 1:9 aloud in French—"If we confess our sins, he is faithful and just and will forgive us our sins and purify us from all unrighteousness"—Anne asked Adeline if she could lead her in a prayer of confession. Adeline agreed, not in French this time but in Dioula, a language closer to her heart.

Upon learning that she did not have a Bible, Anne encouraged Adeline to read the tract we were distributing. It contained Bible verses that would encourage her and give her assurance that God had heard her confession and forgiven her. She'd wandered away from God, guilty and broken, but he'd forgiven her and welcomed her back home again.

Anne encouraged Adeline to live the life of a child of God wherever she was, for her obedient and respectful conduct alone could very well draw her Muslim husband to desire to know Jesus, who had made her heart so beautiful. She counseled her to meditate upon the words of the Bible and pray without ceasing. When we saw Adeline later after handing out other tracts in the area, she was reading the one we'd left behind.

Since we'd promised Adeline that we'd give her a Bible, we made our way back to her roadside stand one more time before leaving the city. Her face radiated that day as she stood behind her simple table, clutching the very Word of God in her hands as the Living Word—Jesus Christ—ruled her heart once again.

Pastor Emmanuel and Anne Yao, missionaries from Cote d'Ivoire to neighboring Burkina Faso

Hungry to Know God

by Heather Webb (Tanzania)

Richard grew up in the Roman Catholic Church. After marrying, he and his wife both fell away from the church. The Church of God pastor in their village visited them faithfully, and eventually they started attending church regularly. Over time, Richard realized that he'd never surrendered his life to Christ. Salvation made him hungry to know God. Discipled by his pastor, he eventually became an elder of his small village church.

When the theological education by extension (TEE) program started in Dodoma in 2008, Richard was encouraged by his pastor, our TEE assistant, to join the class. After completing just two books in the course, Richard has already begun practicing the principles and lessons that he learned. Recently, he preached for the first time on a Sunday morning. In attendance that day was a visitor who was a strong opponent to formal education in spiritual matters. He believed that the Holy Spirit is all that is needed to learn spiritual truths. However, after hearing Richard preach lessons he'd learned through TEE, the visitor's mind was changed. He could see such growth in Richard that he's now a believer in spiritual education.

Tires burning, youth on rampage, and public unrest...

ANOTHER DAY IN PARADISE

by Tim and Colleen Stevenson
(Kampala, Uganda)

In September 2009, central Uganda experienced four days of civil tension and public unrest due to the escalating, ongoing feud between the king of Buganda, the Kabaka tribe, and the Ugandan government. The Buganda people, the largest ethnic group, were angered when the police and military refused to allow their king to travel to another part of the country to attend some prearranged charity events. The rule of law in Uganda is always fragile due to people's beliefs, corruption in the police force, and tribal conflicts.

Colleen and a sponsored child (above); Tim preaching with an interpreter in rural Uganda

Although the country has come a long way in our 23 years here, it is not unusual to have this kind of tension flare up, fueled by poverty, high unemployment rates, and a large youth population. Funny, this same target group is the one we see as the best opportunity for providing hope for the future. Our programs focus on youth through sponsorships, clubs, music festivals, dance and drama, schools, and conventions.

On Thursday afternoon, after a full day in Jinja town, where we interviewed over 70 children sponsored by Furaha (a Canadian program), Colleen and a Canadian delegation of five started back to Kampala. Upon reaching the 25-kilometer point near Mukono town, we merged into a large band of vehicles, all huddling close together. Tires were burning on the road; logs, large boulders, and electrical wires had been strewn around; and youth menacing with stones were on a rampage. Moses, our driver, proceeded to a nearby gas station for refuge, and soon the lot was full of other vehicles all doing the same thing. In hindsight, maybe we shouldn't have fled there due to the road fires, but it was well lit and had a machine gun-armed policeman present. At that time, our relative safety there seemed more important than the danger of explosion.

Tires were burning on the road … and menacing youth with stones were on a rampage.

We remained there for a couple of hours, exchanging near-miss stories with other road refugees and showing off stone-damaged windshields. But the mood changed suddenly when armed police in Land Rovers arrived and announced, "Convoy!" There was immediate response, with every vehicle pulling out in a frenzy, some almost colliding in their dash to follow the armed delegation. We drove through Mukono, racing to keep up and feeling like we were in a Mad Max movie: curtain after curtain of black smoke stung our eyes from burning tires, people on foot ran through the ongoing traffic, and cars were almost flipping when they hit large boulders blocking the road. Meanwhile, we were getting cell phone messages of encouragement from the networks and friends, as well as district leaders phoning to say they were praying for us.

Through it all, we felt God's peace in the car as we prayed for safety. But upon reaching Kampala, the convoy escort disappeared and we were left in a huge traffic jam of hundreds of cars, unable to move. Yet God provided a miraculous opportunity when an armed security group offered to lead us down a back road. We followed this pick-up of well-equipped,

Crowds around Kasubi Tombs threaten to riot after tribal violence damaged the sacred tombs.

exuberant escorts, each cocking his rifle and ready for action. They led us to the main road and waved us on. From there we headed home and had supper. Yawn. It was just another day in paradise!

Yesterday, we planned to enjoy a day with grandmothers at Kasubi Church. Since unrest was still being reported, Tim decided to check it out. He discovered that conditions were unsafe there because Kasubi Church borders some of the king's land—for years a traditional burial site of kings. People in that area were hunkered down to stay out of harm's way while shooting continued all around.

But this is Uganda, so Tim had a cup of tea with those leaders present from northern and central Uganda and the sponsorship staff that had arrived to organize the grandmother program (finding a way through back roads and numerous blocked areas). It was an amazing effort on behalf of the staff of Kasubi. Indeed, they risked their vehicle and even their lives.

Today things are calm: the birds are singing, kids are out on the road, and normalcy has returned because the king decided to stop the bloodshed by ending his travel plans. We are thankful for God's protection and care during these times of uncertainty. Prayer is a powerful tool and we appreciate yours on a daily basis.

My mother set free? I had to see this…

With My Own Eyes

by Mailesi Ndao
(Lusaka, Zambia)

My story begins in the 1990s in a remote area of Zambia—the deep bush of the eastern region—and with my mother who had been demon possessed for many years. Although mum never went to school, when under demonic attack, she spoke fluent English. She used to beat up my dad, and five men could not hold her whenever she came under the influence of these powers. Life was simply unbearable for my parents.

Desperate, they tried seeking help from different witch doctors, but it was to no avail. My mum even made a covenant with the demons by performing rituals and drinking blood from a goat she'd killed with her bare hands. Even worse, she once attended a funeral in the village with her friends. On the way back, she suddenly came under attack and fled, baby on her back, leaving her companions behind. They tried to catch up with her but could not. They did, however, hear a baby crying in the thicket. Following the wails, they found the infant she'd discarded as she ran.

It was during this period that my dad heard of a missionary couple visiting the village through a Zambian named Afeck Lungu (now passed on to be with the Lord). When the missionaries came, my parents were among those who gathered to hear the word of God. It was during this preaching service that my mum heard that there is a name above all names who heals and casts out demons. She responded, was prayed for in the name of Jesus, and was delivered of the demons that had controlled her. As a result, both mum and dad gave their lives to the Lord that day.

Deliverance and salvation was good news to both my parents, but my dad couldn't wait to come and share this miracle with my husband and me. His excitement overflowing, he cycled over 21 kilometers (13 miles) from the village to the place we were and announced, "Your mother has been healed!"

Church leader Mailesi Ndao conducting baptism (above) and preaching in the Avondale Church (right)

"Which witch doctor did you visit this time?" I responded incredulously.

To my surprise, dad answered, "It was not a witch doctor. It was God who came to visit through a missionary couple."

Skeptically, I responded, "A white couple? What were they looking for? There are no tourist attractions in this area."

My dad then narrated the story of what had happened to both mum and him and invited us to come and see for ourselves; the missionaries were coming back. I traveled with my husband and a few friends, curious to meet this couple and check them out. I had to see with my own eyes. Admittedly, I was doubtful, especially about the white couple. (I'd gone to a school where my teachers were white, and they never shook our hands, no matter how hard we worked and studied.)

It took us from 6:00 AM until 4:00 PM to walk the distance to the village. When we finally arrived, I saw a white woman among black ladies. When the women saw us, they immediately welcomed us. But it was the white woman who made the biggest impression on me. I knew something was different about her when she opened her arms to me and held me, even though I was sweaty, tired, and surely a sight. It was the first time I'd come so closely face to face with a white woman, and I saw nothing but love. I learned that her name was Marion Hoffman. She and her husband Stanley were the missionaries who'd shown up in a village that didn't know white faces.

That evening, there was another service under a tree. Sitting on the grass, I heard the message that changed my life. "Behold the old has gone, the new has come!" the missionary told us. It was as if he was preaching directly to me, and I was one of the people who gave my life to Jesus that night. (You don't know what pieces God had to pick up and put together in that moment to bring me to him.)

From that moment until today, I tell everyone that this is the best thing that's ever happened to me. I was never the same again, and like my dad, I began sharing about Jesus and his saving grace with everyone I met. That's about all my husband and I knew about the Lord, but we wanted to tell the story of what had happened to my mum and how God had changed our lives, so we started gathering people together for worship in our home. The next time the Hoffmans visited, they had another church to open—the first Church of God congregation in our area. I'm so grateful the missionaries came to my village because I'm a product of missions.

Mailesi Ndao translating for Stanley Hoffman in an outdoor church service in Zambia

Battling both God and timidity, I was…

AN UNLIKELY SERVANT

by Yao Kaumé Allen*
(Yamoussoukro, Côte d'Ivoire)

Yao Kaumé Allen, brick maker and God's servant

The Bible is full of amazing stories. Because mine could be among them, I want to give glory to God for what he has done for me.

Before I came to Christ, I opposed anyone who spoke of God or Jesus. Everyone knew I was someone who couldn't be convinced of any need of him. That was until 1998, when I became sick with an ulcer. In spite of all the medical treatments, the problem persisted. A neighbor friend who attends the Church of God in Yamoussoukro assured me that God could heal me. I agreed to see the pastor of her church; he was known to pray for the sick. It was the first time I'd ever been to a church.

The pastor attested that God was capable of healing me. He then asked if I believed in God. I responded that God existed, but his healing me simply by prayer was a stretch! Still, he prayed for me and asked me to return again for more prayer. I began to attend this church where, because of the pastor's prayers, my pain began to lessen until I was totally well. God convinced me he is able to heal when we ask.

Following the teaching and preaching from the Word of God, I came to understand my sins. I decided to abandon them and accept Jesus as my Savior, and I was baptized thereafter.

From the very beginning, the brothers and sisters in Christ—even the pastor—saw potential in me to be a servant of God. But when I considered

* Translated from French by Kay Critser

Yao Kaumé Allen and TEE in the village

their zeal and abilities, I felt this was impossible. I always replied that I couldn't possibly be a servant of God. I was very shy and found it difficult to speak before a group of people. In elementary school, I didn't speak in class even when I knew the answers to the questions. Whenever my name was placed on the list of talkers, the teachers would ignore it because they knew I wouldn't be caught speaking at any time. I was like that throughout my high school years. Though I belonged to a community youth society, I didn't take part in the group because I saw myself as the least of men, eternally timid. No matter what anyone said, for me it was no, no, and no. I couldn't be a servant of God.

One day, however, the pastor said he wanted me to try leading the worship service. As the day drew near, fear began building in me. I prayed and asked God to release me from the assignment, but he didn't. In spite of my handicaps (not only was I shy, but I didn't know how to sing), I took the microphone and began to direct with the help of some sisters in Christ who led the singing. Afterwards the pastor told me that the Lord would help me do even better in the days to come. Sometime later, he approached me about preaching. With the Lord's help, I tried and little by little preaching became natural to me.

During this time, I began studying in a Bible extension program. Through it, I learned much about God, Jesus, and the Holy Spirit and gained understanding of the Bible and how to present it. This continues to transform my preaching even today, just as I've also been transformed through becoming active in the local youth program. There, I was elected treasurer, eventually leading me to youth involvement nationally.

As I reflect on how God has brought me to my present level of ministry, I marvel at how he can take someone like me, who considered himself incapable of leadership, and place me where I am today. Truly, with God all things are possible. I'm a living example.

A missionary reminisces with joy and tears.

FOUR EGGS OF GRATITUDE

by Glenna Phippen
(Edmonton, Alberta, Canada)

Glenna Phippen receiving eggs at her farewell

What an incredible six years it has been! As I sit in London's Heathrow Airport and reflect upon what has been an amazing journey, tears come easily. I am leaving Uganda—the people and work that I love—to return home to Canada.

Seven- and a-half-years ago, when I committed to the Lord to go to the mission field, I didn't know what my future would hold. But I trusted God as never before in my life. Today I can testify that he has been faithful even beyond my expectations. His leading and guiding were evident from the very beginning, and he has seen me through this journey. Raising support, which I dreaded and wanted to avoid, turned out to be a huge blessing to me. The needed prayers and financial assistance soon began to flow, and it has continued to this day in more than full measure. I've been humbled by the confidence and trust in me and can only thank our awesome God again and again.

I can surely speak of the Lord's wonderful love to me when I was "in a besieged city." First of all, moving to Kampala necessitated lifestyle adjustments. No longer did I feel safe driving alone at night. My social life was severely curtailed, a difficult and lonely adjustment. Several break-in attempts occurred where I lived. Even in broad daylight, a thief reached through my open car window and ripped a gold chain from my neck. (Theft is a big problem, as high unemployment leads to desperate acts for survival. Prisons are full of people, especially the young, who are guilty of stealing food or cell phones, which they can sell for money to buy food.) Just last week, I was awakened in the night by a man's screaming. He'd attempted to steal a *boda boda* (motorcycle) and was being chased by an angry mob. Guards from nearby compounds intervened, saving the would-be thief from death. Mob justice is swift and sure in Uganda.

My main desire when I went to Uganda was to share God's hope, healing, and love.

In a country where the political climate is sensitive and changes daily, I've experienced tear gas, the cross fire of gunshots, and crowds of people throwing stones at the car and blocking traffic. I've been in several car accidents, thankfully escaping injury each time. On at least three occasions, I was threatened with arrest and prison for infractions such as not wearing a seat belt, speeding, having staff working without licenses, and because of a medication error made by a staff member. In Uganda, daily life is full of uncertainty and drama.

And then there is AIDS. The prevalence of Ugandans infected with HIV/AIDS is reportedly 7 percent of the population. However, frontline health care work convinces me that it is much higher. Recently, as I met with a support group of women living with HIV, I witnessed some of their countenances change from despair to hope and joy as I taught them songs of encouragement and faith in Christ. The songs were soothing medicine to their sad, weary, and aching hearts.

Not long ago, I drove a young girl named Night to see her mother, who was dying of AIDS in a refugee camp in northern Uganda. Her father had already succumbed to AIDS; soon their daughter will be an orphan. I was able to pray with Night and her mother and give the mother medicine

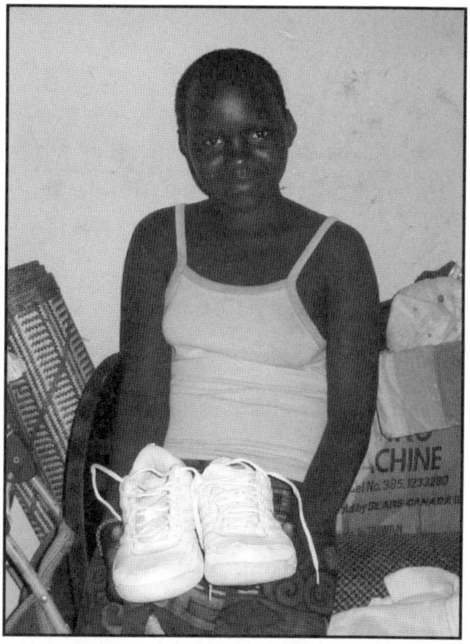

Night and Christmas shoes from Glenna

for her terrible cough from tuberculosis. How thankful I was when the Lord provided a sponsor for Night so that she can continue school. In the past year, she has learned English, accepted Christ as her Savior, and even begun to smile—something that took an especially long time. Last night, as I left for the airport, she hugged me and whispered in my ear, "Thank you, Auntie. God bless you." Do you understand my tears as I think about Night here in Heathrow Airport?*

At a farewell party at Nampunge Health Center, I was blessed and humbled by the words, gifts, and appreciation of the staff, church leaders, and community members who gathered. An elderly Muslim gentleman came to me and declared, "Dear Sister, I give you four eggs." Inside the envelope he held was enough money to buy four eggs. What a gift of love! We'd met in the Health Center when his two-year-old grandson passed away. He and his wife allowed me to pray with them as they cried over the little child's body, and I gave them money to transport the little bundle home to their village for burial. Health care is about so much more than just medicine.

I thank God for allowing me to be his hands and feet and to share his heart in Uganda for these short six years. He has blessed my efforts. Today the Church of God Medical Department is an even more vital evangelistic tool in providing healing and hope to the nation. My prayer is to continue helping by inspiring others to prayerfully and financially support the health-care ministry. My main desire when I went to Uganda was to share God's hope, healing, and love. As I leave, I'm happy to know that in some small measure I've done that.

* Night's mother passed away on January 17, 2010.

All her fingers fit neatly across my thumbnail.

A Miracle Named Rhea

by Rochelle Doyle
(Auckland, New Zealand)

We all have burdens to carry, hard situations that challenge us in our lives. But no matter how dark the night, the psalmist knew that "rejoicing comes in the morning." Like David, we declare to the Lord, "You turned my wailing into dancing; you removed my sackcloth and clothed me with joy, that my heart may sing to you and not be silent. O Lord my God, I will give you thanks forever" (Psalm 30:11–12).

Our recent challenge began when I was told, at 10 weeks into my pregnancy, that I was miscarrying. It intensified through the subsequent journey leading to the birth of our baby girl, Rhea, on January 21, 2009. She was extremely premature at 25 gestational weeks and weighed only one pound seven ounces. All her fingers, with their fragile translucent skin, fit neatly across my thumbnail. That's how small she was.

"When it's dark enough, you can see the stars." These words were printed on a brochure in the Neonatal Intensive Care Unit (NICU) where our baby girl lay for months. It should have said, "When it's dark enough, the light of God's love and mercy shines even brighter." Events had catapulted us from a comfortable daily life of work, two children, the mortgage, the cat, and being Christians to this new reality. Now God isn't just head knowledge and a calm nodding in agreement for us. He's so much more—ever present, ever real, and ever vibrant to us!

I could talk about the darkness of the months before Rhea's birth and the challenges that continue even today, but isn't the light shining through it much more beautiful? I could talk about the siege as every day new and even more frightening challenges were thrown at us, but isn't God's mercy through it all so much more memorable?

Don't get me wrong. This has been no easy ride; it still isn't. Our daughter was exceptionally tiny, resuscitated at birth, and battling chronic

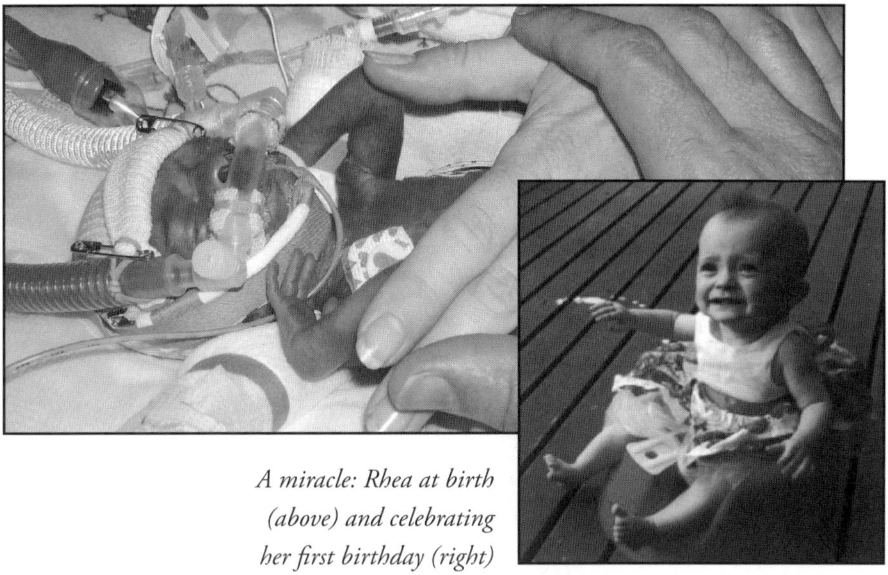

A miracle: Rhea at birth (above) and celebrating her first birthday (right)

lung disease. She had a lumbar puncture within days of her birth, and yet it was over a week before she got her first cuddle. We've been through eye surgery, apneas, ventilation, tube feeding, bradycardia, blood transfusions, bone density issues, and more. For months before and after Rhea was born, we faced the fearful whisper that today we might lose our wee baby. It was a terror that could easily overcome me. But every time I battled between trusting God and slipping towards hysteria and accusations against him, he mercifully comforted us.

We received prayers, Bible references, and visits just when we needed these most. Through these we felt God's comfort and we witnessed the deliberate execution of his plans. Many times we read a particular e-mail or received a specific prayer and sat together marveling at the powerful words and their amazingly perfect timing.

It's easy to praise God when all is good, but we want to praise and thank God for his blessings during this dark time of siege. In fact, so much of this experience has been about blessings. Here are a few that God showered upon us through this trial. They are the evidence that God answers prayers.

- The day my water broke I was at a hospital appointment for a planned iron infusion. What better place to be? Otherwise I'd have been at home with my toddler and no car.

- My midwife for the first three nights in hospital (prior to giving birth to Rhea) was a Christian woman I knew. In the early hours of the morning when I was most scared, she held my hand and reminded me of God's hand over the situation.
- Steve (my husband) got to stay nights in the hospital, sleeping on a mattress on the floor beside my bed. The staff kindly sneaked in extra meals for him every day.
- After my water broke, praise God that I didn't go home on the eleventh day of false labor, as I wanted. The very next day I delivered (although a nurse first thought it was more false labor). Had I been at home, both Rhea and I could have died.
- The high risk specialist arrived just in time and identified that it wasn't false labor. I was already eight centimeters dilated; she could see Rhea's arm! By then, it was too late for a Caesarean. As a result, I recovered more quickly and could hug and lift my boys sooner.
- Afterwards, the specialist told us that normally she'd have started her rounds at the other end of the ward. "Wasn't it lucky we started at your end?" she asked. No, it was God.
- Steve made it to the hospital in time to be with me during Rhea's birth despite having gone home that morning to do a few jobs.
- The surgeon who recommended that we do no intervention also gave us the most critical advice. "If you're going to give birth naturally, push like you've never pushed before." With those words ringing in his ears, Steve yelled at me to push when I didn't want to, so Rhea was born very quickly, without birthing complications or distress.
- Doctors resolved my complications after birth without the hysterectomy they had wheeled me into surgery expecting to do.
- Rhea's birth was perfectly timed as medical staff confirmed that my placenta was small and ill. If she had stayed inside me any longer, she would have suffered. God knew the right timing even though we'd thought it would be better to delay the birth.
- At this stage, Rhea doesn't have any of the major health issues that preemies are prone to have. She's used a ventilator only one day, and she amazes doctors by needing only minimal breathing assistance, remarkable for a baby born so early and as small as she.

- I arrived one day to visit Rhea at just the right time; she was choking on a blocked ventilator tube (the one day she was on it). The medical staff hadn't noticed; they were looking at the monitors, not at her, trying to figure out why her stats were bad while she was gasping for breath, unnoticed. I saw it as soon as I came in.
- Unsaved friends have seen our faith in God, giving us many opportunities to share. Not only this, but our nine-year-old son has witnessed firsthand our trust in God and the power of prayer, and he has shared with his friends too.
- Today, at 10 months old, Rhea continues to wow her specialists. She's responded exceptionally to eye surgery, exceeded social and intellectual development milestones, digested solids readily without issue, and she defies the statistics.

Throughout this journey, God's gems of blessing (and these are just a few) shone brightly among the difficulty, and they lead us through.

A dear friend asked recently about my faith now with all that's happened; she expected we'd be questioning a God she doesn't believe in. Imagine her surprise when I told her that our faith is stronger than ever, that through this, God has revealed himself like never before and that we have so much to be thankful for.

We also have a deeper understanding of God. We know firsthand now how God hears the groanings of our hearts when we can't even utter words and how he responds with mercy and love. We also understand God's love for us far more. Before Rhea was born, we loved her and planned for her, and we would have taken her pain in the blink of an eye to save her. God's love is even greater than that.

In these intervening months, our reliance on God also has grown stronger. People see Rhea at home, growing and getting stronger, and for them everything seems fine. But God sees the difficulties that remain and feels the fears we still face, and he will continue to walk alongside us no matter how long the journey.

God knows what is happening in your life. God's hand controlled Rhea's birth, his mercy took us through it, and his plan continues to unfold. His hand is also over your life, and he will give you unimaginable love, comfort, mercy, and grace if you will accept it. We pray that God is praised through our story and that the Holy Spirit speaks to you through it.

God prepared me for the news no one wants to hear.

Sit Still, My Daughter

by Cheryl Johnson Barton
(Tokyo, Japan)

I have never heard God's voice, but one day he spoke to me so clearly that I can describe his voice. It is the voice of love and compassion, the voice of peace in the middle of a storm, and the voice I will follow for the rest of my life.

It was the morning of September 4, 2009. The theme verse for that day's Bible readings surprised me: "Be still, my daughter." I couldn't imagine where that was found in the Bible, so I looked up the reference: Ruth 3:18. Surely I'd read it before, but it had never spoken to me as it did after I compared this version (New King James) with the rendering in my usual translation (New International), that declared, "Wait, my daughter."

Immediately I was struck by the feeling difference between the two versions. The word *waiting* prompted me to visualize the start of a

Cheryl Barton, recovering from surgery, and Don Deena Johnson, her sister, visiting a Japanese garden

horse race. Mounted horses wait in chutes for the buzzer to sound, the gates to bang open, bolting forward as the race begins. Although waiting, there is no stillness anywhere. Muscles are taut with expectation and there is impatient movement, even though controlled by the small confines of the chute and the mounted jockey. Amid some pawing of the ground and tension-filled snorting, horses and riders are completely alert as they focus, not on waiting, but on the moment they will be set free to run with the wind. There is absolutely no resting in this kind of waiting.

"Sit still, my daughter" is entirely different. I pictured sitting with my mother in church so many years ago as a child. If I jiggled my legs or swung them back and forth under the pew, she soon would put her hand on my leg and say quietly, "Sit still, Cheryl." What she meant was, "Stop jiggling and be quiet. It's time for church; later you can do other things. But for now, just be still and in this moment."

I also remembered her hand on my tiny, feverish forehead. "Lay still, Cheryl, and rest," she'd soothe. It didn't matter what I should have been doing, wished I were doing, or wanted to be doing. The immediate call was for stillness in the moment. And through this, healing would come on its own schedule.

After meditating on the passage that morning, I wrote in my journal: "Stillness goes with quietness (both of body and spirit). It implies peacefulness, rest, and renewal—all these things I am seeking, Lord God. And so I hear you this morning, 'Sit still, my daughter.' I will remain quietly and obediently in this moment, not anticipating anything to come—just reveling in your loving presence. Thank you for speaking so directly to my heart this morning."

I had no way of knowing that later that very day my respiratory doctor would say to me, "I suspect your renal cell carcinoma has returned."

At first, sitting on a blue-gray Naugahyde chair, awaiting the results of a CT scan ordered to confirm or deny the doctor's suspicions, I felt numb—not good, not bad, not anything. But slowly the impact of his words began invading the protective shell that held me, and suddenly my mind was the lead car in a NASCAR race. No longer was I in that hospital waiting area. I was now three-plus months ahead wondering whether I'd see Christmas in December or the birth of my granddaughter in January.

As my thoughts teetered on panic, I heard the gentle, calming voice of God, "Sit still, my daughter." Suddenly the tension and fear disappeared as I focused, not on the future, but on that very moment and on God's presence with me in it. Circumstances had changed, even dramatically. But the One who said, "Never will I leave you; never will I forsake you," was also the One who "is the same yesterday and today and forever."* And in that moment, I heard his voice and I was comforted.

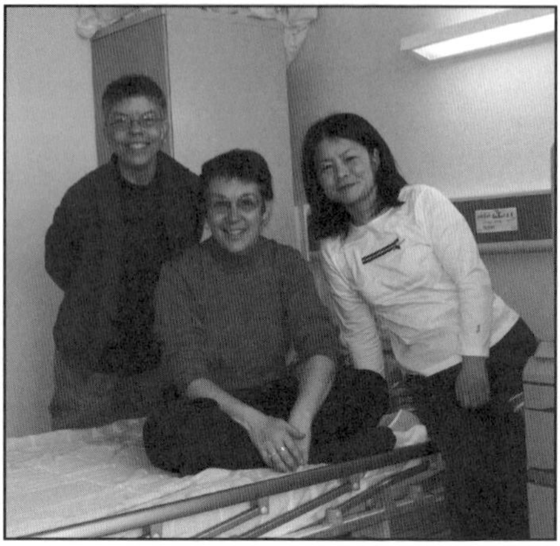

Cheryl, in the hospital bed, and prayer partners

"Sit still, my daughter," he reminded me. And with gratitude overflowing, I answered, "Yes, Father, I will obey."

* Hebrews 13:5, 8

God's Investment Plan

by Julie Kurrle (Paraguay)

When we dedicated our 1988 "Blue Cruiser" to the Lord's service in 2002, we had no idea that we would use it to transport hundreds of people to youth and pastors' retreats, visit countless families, and even save lives by driving people to the hospital when there were no ambulances available.

Usually cars depreciate in value. However, God's economy isn't the same as that of the world. We sold our car for $2,300 more than we bought it for and with 200,000 more miles. We are learning that what we dedicate to the Lord continues to multiply in longevity, quality, and value. Much better than what you'll find in CDs or the stock market are the investments that you have in God's service, and you won't need cash for clunkers.

How a Hindu met Christ on a…

Bus Journey to Hope

by Leaderwell Pohsngap
(Shillong, Meghalaya, India)

Hours on airplanes, trains, buses, and in cars wasn't written into my job description. But as international director of Global LEAD Alliance, I seem to spend much of my time traveling from one training seminar or meeting to another. But this isn't all bad.

On July 24, 2009, I took a bus from Mumbai to Pune, India, to conduct a half-day seminar on our philosophy of leadership development. I was also to attend the twenty-fifth anniversary of the relocation of Union Biblical Seminary to its present campus. (I was invited as one of the former school presidents.) Next to me in the bus sat a man younger than I. After some time, we struck up a conversation. I learned that Vivek, who lives in Mumbai, is a detergent consultant with big hotels. I also learned that he is a Hindu. He was on his way to meet with his clients. I introduced myself as a consultant on leadership development. I told him how we try to develop people of character, that we do this on Christian principles, and that I am a follower of Jesus Christ. Vivek responded that he also reveres Jesus Christ. He was very interested in what I am doing and agreed with me about the need for leaders of integrity everywhere. As we parted, I gave him my calling card. Vivek asked me to pray for him, and I promised I would.

I did pray and continue to do so. Shortly after our bus trip together, Vivek sent me a surprising request. "I know you have direct communion with Jesus Christ," he wrote, "so please relay to him what I need and secure it from him. May he be with us forever."

Responding, I wrote back, "Vivek, yes I am in communion with Jesus Christ, but I do not have an exclusive communion with him. All those who believe in him have the same opportunity. I suggest that you pray to him too. Ask him to help you understand who he is and invite him to become your personal Savior. He is more than willing to help you.

A bus in India bound for heaven

Once you accept him, he will definitely help you and give you wisdom to deal with your problems. Besides your own prayer, try to get a Bible and read it. I can also connect you with believers in Christ in Mumbai, if you so desire."

In his return e-mail, Vivek declared, "Indeed, there was a [divine] plan behind our meeting. Yesterday, I discovered that a driver who works for the laundry where I am a consultant is a devout follower of Jesus. He drove me to various places for some office-related work yesterday and today. During our time together, he filled my mind with some great revelations. He shared how God's grace and peace are available for me and urged me to forgive those who have wronged me and to show them compassion by praying for their welfare. I've noticed that this driver is so forgiving and compassionate; even towards those who cause him harm, he's not vindictive. I'm learning and gaining a lot in his company. He's offered to give me a copy of the Bible. Of course, it will be wonderful to get connected with believers in Mumbai."

Eagerly, I called my Christian friend in Mumbai. He was happy to get in touch with Vivek, whom God loves very much. God has been using many of us—myself, the driver, and my friend in Mumbai—to introduce Jesus to Vivek and his family.

I'm reminded of Paul's letter to the Corinthians. When they squabbled about who belonged to Paul and who belonged to Apollos, Paul wrote to them, "Apollos and I are merely servants who helped you to have faith. It was the Lord who made it all happen. I planted the seeds, Apollos watered them, but God made them sprout and grow" (1 Corinthians 3:5–7 CEV).

I'm grateful to be part of the team that has planted and watered seeds in Vivek's heart. Now I'm watching expectantly to see how God will bring Vivek to faith and eternal hope in Christ.

A month's rainfall in one day spelled...

Disaster in the Philippines

by Linda Mason
(Anderson, Indiana)

Micah Joy Formaran's family faced the same torrential rains as all Filipinos living on the main island of Luzon when Typhoon Ketsana bore down on the Philippines in late September 2009. Drenching metro Manila with 17.9 inches of rain on September 26, the typhoon—called Ondoy in the Philippines—brought a month's worth of rainfall in a single day. The most rain ever recorded in 24 hours toppled and washed away homes in an instant and stranded thousands of victims on rooftops throughout the city. But rural areas were not spared either. In some localities, flood waters were 20 feet deep, destroying rice paddies and depriving many families of income for the next six months. Before its reign of terror ended, Typhoon Ketsana had moved on across Southeast Asia, spreading similar havoc in Vietnam, Cambodia, and Laos.

But not everything was the same for the Formaran family and Micah Joy, one of the 731 children sponsored by Grace Family Helper Project (Children of Promise) in the Philippines. In the midst of everything, her mother gave birth to a baby sister, Micah Ella. Miraculously, both mother and baby came through the harrowing experience without further trauma than the typhoon itself unleashed.

While the storm was downing banana trees and caving in the back wall of Santa Cruz Church of God, the church Micah's father pastors southeast of Manila, the family huddled in Micah Joy's bedroom. Each succeeding gust of wind or onslaught of rain claimed a bit more of their house. In the end, part of the roof and one wall were gone, but the family was safe and praising God.

Last November, less than two months after the disaster, I had the opportunity to visit the Philippines. Along with Ofelia Viray, executive director of the Grace Family Project, we surveyed seven of the thirteen areas where Children of Promise serves through Church of God congregations. Even then, there were a few houses in these areas still inaccessible, either due to standing water or knee-deep mud. I tried especially hard not to think about what might be in that filthy water—or the mud, for that matter. After all, we were only visiting, but these victims were living in the midst of it all. I certainly wanted to do all I could to help.

My heart was especially broken when we visited an area north of Manila. There several of our Children of Promise families had been relocated by the government from their shanties along the railroad tracks in Manila. Their uprooting had come only shortly before the typhoon. Not only had they lost their support community—friends, family, and church—in the forced move, but now they had also lost what few household goods and personal effects they owned when the river nearby flooded their new homes almost to the ceiling. Their grief was palpable, and I longed to be able to say something to comfort and assure them that everything would be fine soon. But I noted that the river that had brought such despair upon them was only half a block away. When would it flood again? And what would be their desperation then? I fought back the tears.

Despite the devastation that was still apparent everywhere, I rejoiced that none of our children had lost their lives and that 24 family homes already had been restored. (Typically, repairs were made with plywood sheets for walls and galvanized iron sheets for roofs.) Thirty-two family homes still needed immediate attention, and I suspected that many more homes would also need repairs in the weeks to come.

It was a blessing to me that on the day we visited Pastor Formaran and his family, galvanized sheeting and plywood were delivered so the repair work could begin. "We prayed for safety when the storm came. And we prayed for materials for our house after the storm. We are grateful for your gifts," he thanked us with heartfelt words.

In addition to seeing some repair work in progress, we also talked with families about their experiences during the storms. (More heavy rain, causing more flooding and landslides, came within a week of Ketsana.) We were able to help distribute relief supplies to our children and their families. Contents of the packages included food (canned meats, rice, Milo), a large plastic bowl to wash dishes and bathe in, a sleeping mat, a cooking pot, pails with lids, plates, cups and silverware, dish towels,

Washing out what was salvaged after Ketsana (left); not all sponsored children's homes were accessible (below).

plastic storage boxes, bathing and laundry soap, clothing (new and used), medicines (as needed), school supplies (paper, pens, pencils, back packs), and toiletries. Some also received rubber boots and blankets.

"My heart bleeds for the people of the Philippines," Dr. Viray shared during a phone conversation as the scars from the disaster were becoming apparent. Not only had flooding swept away some of our children's homes, severely damaged most, and caused massive loss of personal effects, but the offices of Grace Family Helper Project were flooded, sustaining damage to food supplies for the children, records, and office equipment.

As we continue monitoring and supporting relief efforts, the story that emerges out of this disaster is the resilience of the Filipino people in the face of disaster. I came away from my visit truly inspired and humbled by the dedication of the Grace Family Helper staff, who despite their own suffering went out day after day to help meet other people's needs. Their own homes had been damaged, and they were still sleeping on wet spongy beds. Still, they were concerned most of all for the sponsored children. I was inspired by these dedicated servants of God who daily lay down their lives to assist the people God has sent to them—namely, the children of the Philippines. And I am privileged to have shared with them and learned from them.

We have confidence, no matter life's uncertainties.

And God Is in It

by Jodie Ackerman
(Montaign Noire, Haiti)

Most of the time, we go around "doing life" and convincing ourselves that what we are doing is important and that what we have is really ours, gained by ourselves. But that can all change in a few seconds. We have been vividly reminded of this since Haiti's catastrophic earthquake of January 12, 2010. Homes, family and friends, businesses, and life as we know it have all been taken away. But oh how real is the stuff that remains! It is truly not a pat answer to quote Romans 8:28 (God works together for good) in the aftermath of this tragedy because we've already seen him working in so many ways, and we wait expectantly to see what he will accomplish in the future.

My personal story (and, of course, there are thousands) follows. It had been a typical school day: teaching kindergarten, eating lunch with the children, working in my classroom in the afternoon, and giving piano lessons after school. I had everything ready for the next day. John, my husband, had picked up his sister Caroline and her friend Claudette from the airport and was out with them, so I planned to stop at the grocery store on the way home. I had a long shopping list, but I also enjoying visiting with friends who were also there.

Finished, my daughter Jessica and I checked out, loaded the car, and headed up the main road of Delmas. When the car suddenly began to swerve back and forth, I told her we must have a flat. Then I noticed that other cars were also swerving around. We stopped, realizing it was an earthquake, and waited out the shaking that seemed to last forever. (Actually, it was less than a minute.) There was much noise, and screaming people were running in the street. I noticed a lot of dust in the air ahead of us and wondered why the traffic didn't start moving. Then the shaking began again. Although crying, Jessica managed to call several friends and John, confirming they were all right.

Finally, I decided to change course, choosing whatever roads seemed clear to get us home. As I drove, I saw a few collapsed walls, but these all seemed to be property walls rather than building parts. We finally arrived home shaken, but okay. A large shelf by the door had fallen and dumped its contents everywhere, so we picked it all up, stacking everything on the living room floor. We tried making phone calls, but contact was very spotty. Finally, a friend contacted us to say she was online with our daughter Jacquie (in the United States), who wanted to know about us. So we asked her to call family to tell them we were fine. That was the last phone contact we would have for a while.

Haitians surveying earthquake damage

We then discovered we had no Internet. However, we still had television reception; that was how we started learning about the extent of the quake. But that first night we got very little information except that the magnitude of the earthquake was 7.0. When our landlord came to check on us, he told us of several places that had collapsed, including Caribbean Market, where Jessica and I had shopped on the way home.

We ate supper, watched some news, and eventually went to bed, but I didn't sleep well that night. Every aftershock—and there were many—brought me up and out of bed. Part of the night we just stood on the balcony, shivering and looking down on Port-au-Prince, wondering what had really happened there.

As light dawned the morning after, we used binoculars to try to see below us. While we couldn't see much, we noticed that a large house and some smaller homes on the hillside had collapsed. We were shocked when John realized we could no longer see the famous Hotel Montana. Finally around noon, John decided to check on a few people; Jessica and

Caroline went with him. While they were out, they saw some damage and heard of much more.

That evening our Internet was back, so we busily contacted many people in the States. By the next morning we had phone service too, although it wasn't very consistent. Thursday we stayed home, worked on communications, and tried to figure out what to do next. It felt like we should be doing something, though we didn't know what. But we knew we couldn't just keep driving around town because we didn't know when we'd be able to get fuel again.

Friday we drove down to Delmas to see my school. We also went to Tabarre, where John works with Heartline Ministries, to check on them and learn what they were planning to do. The damage we saw was shocking. Places that were part of our everyday lives were either completely gone or badly damaged. Many big buildings were down, while others were standing undamaged as if nothing had happened. We learned that Heartline would be starting a medical clinic on Monday, so John helped with the planning and promised to be there. We also learned that several groups were coming in to the school and that I was to clear out my classroom so it could be used for other things.

Five days after the quake, we met with a very small group of our church family to share and pray together. We also saw more of what was happening at the school. We managed to get a few gallons of diesel to keep our generator running for a few hours a day and made plans to get Caroline and Claudette out of Haiti on MFI (Mission Flight International) on Monday.

That day, Jessica and I worked at school while John went to the clinic. It was sad to put away all my things, probably for the rest of the school year. I grieved for the short time I'd been with my class and for the kids who never got to say goodbye to each other. We also made the difficult decision for Jessica to leave Haiti for a break from the stress. She left the next day on MFI after waiting at the airport for over seven hours.

Tuesday and Wednesday, I went with John to Heartline Ministries. I'm not a medical person, but there was plenty for me to do. I unpacked supplies, sorted and put everything away, did some interpreting for the doctors and nurses who'd come to help, ran up and down the stairs to get things from the pharmacy they'd set up, and when possible, worked on the Internet. They were tiring days and we arrived home late, but at least we felt that we were doing something to help.

After the earthquake, Jodie Ackerman and her one-room schoolhouse class

For the next two days, I was at the school to help in the command center. I was amazed at the changes that had already taken place there. Furniture had been moved and the lower half of the campus had been taken over by the U.S. Army. The elementary library now housed the school office, and most elementary classrooms were being used by relief teams for living quarters. My classroom was completely different, with things moved and stacked haphazardly. I swallowed and tried not to think about how I'd ever find everything and organize it again.

One classroom was reserved for the command center, for communications and coordination for all the relief efforts and teams. People were coming and going, with many groups being transported to work locations each day. It had become an enormous operation. I've spent most of the past two days in this command center. There I met some amazing people from various nations, all working together to help Haitians. I saw several friends from years past in Haiti who'd come back to help, and I talked to others who wanted to come. It was overwhelming, but in a good way.

What does the future hold? We don't know, of course. But I believe that God is going to do incredible things in Haiti in the months and years to come. There are plans taking shape to begin school for those of our students still on island with our staff that remains. I'll be part of that, probably teaching the lower elementary children in a one-room schoolhouse-type setting. There are still many unknowns to life here, but it is a good reminder that the future is always unknown anyway. And God is in it.

I practiced for the ministry in my mother's garden.

Tale of the Toothpaste Box Caskets

by Sheldon L. Anderson
(St. Ann, Jamaica)

I grew up in a rural community in Jamaica and started attending the Church of God as a young child. It was the church located nearest our home, and it was also where my mother was a member. I experienced life as an average Jamaican youth and was baptized at the age of nine. Growing up in the church, it was natural for me to participate in most church programs and activities ranging from playing musical instruments to leading committees and boards.

But all this wasn't just youthful busyness; I had a call on my life. The evidence of this call is found in my pastime activities as a child. Looking back, I can say that my life now as a minister of the gospel was played out in my mother's garden. This was the place where I often conducted mock funeral services using toothpaste boxes as caskets. For mock weddings, I placed two bottles beside each other, and these bottles would repeat their vows under my instruction. I would then move to my mother's bathtub to carry out baptismal services.

As I became a teenager, however, my interest in these activities faded somewhat. After high school, I started charting my own path and became preoccupied with my future career. While awaiting my high school comprehensive examination results, I actively pursued several courses that would help prepare me for my future and eagerly took university entrance exams. It seemed everything was going according to my plans.

But the day my comprehensive results came, my hopes were dashed; I had failed them all. The rest of my siblings had been successful in their examinations and were pursuing college and university courses. I was left behind; I was the one to fail. This thought haunted me mercilessly until one day, while I was in a fasting service, the Lord confronted me as I cried tears of despondency. He told me clearly that had I been successful,

I now would be focused on my own path; he had other plans for me instead.

Gratefully, after that very clear and powerful encounter with the Lord, I began to experience an increasingly strong desire to enter the ministry. It was encouraging when my spiritual fathers and friends affirmed this call upon my life. Finally the day came when I yielded myself totally to God. No longer would I live for my plans; from then on, I was dedicated wholly to God's.

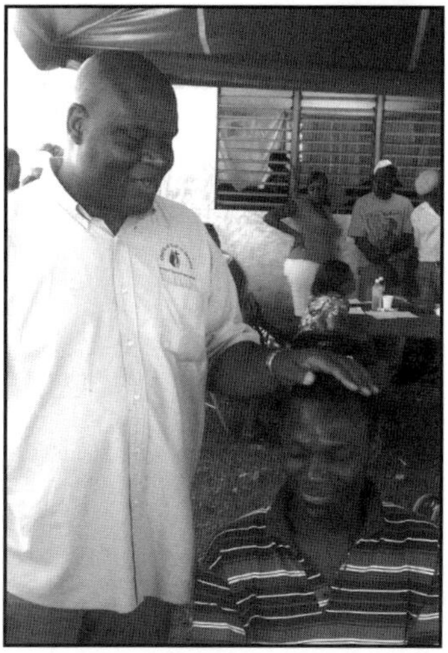

Sheldon Anderson ministering outside the church

Pursuing God's call, I enrolled in Jamaica's Leadership Training Institute in 1995. The curriculum offered a range of courses which I pursued successfully. Having had only a high school education up to then, I was enlightened through courses in biblical studies as well as other areas such as psychology. The standard of work was high, and the variety of courses prepared me for my ministry today as pastor of two congregations: Bonham Spring and Prosper Hall Churches of God in the parish of St. Ann.

In the 11 years since I graduated from the Leadership Training Institute, the Lord has blessed my ministry wonderfully. The first congregation I began leading has grown significantly both in numbers and quality of membership. Each department of the church—Sunday school, youth fellowship, and women's and men's groups—has developed, and many lay leaders have been trained to lead ministry teams. Another high point came during the eighth year of my ministry when this congregation planted a new church. Some of the leaders in the mother church were transferred to the new body to offer leadership under my supervision.

These reflections echo my gratitude to the staff and support team at the Leadership Training Institute. The educational foundation that was laid in my life there has helped me through God to build not only church buildings but also lives of men and women. Today, I experience fulfillment and joy knowing that I am fulfilling my purpose; I am in the right place doing what God wants for me. To God be the glory.

As I stood over my young patient, I found myself talking with God.

The Acuity Level Principle

by John Ackerman
(Montaign Noire, Haiti)

Recently I've been amazed at the patients I'm seeing on a regular basis. While working as a nursing supervisor in a small Indiana hospital prior to coming to Haiti in 1986, I became very aware of the concept of the acuity level of the average patient. We occasionally went through times when the acuity level of our little hospital would go up rather rapidly—meaning that our nursing staff was taking care of sicker and sicker patients while the number of people in our care stayed relatively the same. I never imagined that I would ever deal with this same principle in Haiti. I am.

A couple of weeks ago, I recall a 26-year-old male patient who was carried in and lifted onto my examination table. As I stood over him, I suddenly realized that I was in totally over my head. This young man was very sick.

Already that morning, I'd examined two babies unlike those I usually see—little ones with kwashiorkor (protein deficiency malnutrition that causes tiny bodies to swell). These two babies were different, and there was a good chance that one or both of them wouldn't make it.

And now, here was one who should have been in the prime of his life. As I stood over my young patient, I found myself talking with God. I wondered if he was allowing the acuity level of this little village health clinic to rise beyond the knowledge of his servant. You see, I always asked him to give me a place to serve where I would know without doubt that any good I might be able to accomplish there was because of his working through me rather than because of my ability to treat sick people. God granted me that wish here at the Prospere Clinic in rural Haiti.

Recently I find that I must rely on the increased sensitivity that God gives me, along with the knowledge that he is standing there with me as

A little girl suffering from kwashiorkor (right); John Ackerman using his nursing skills (below)

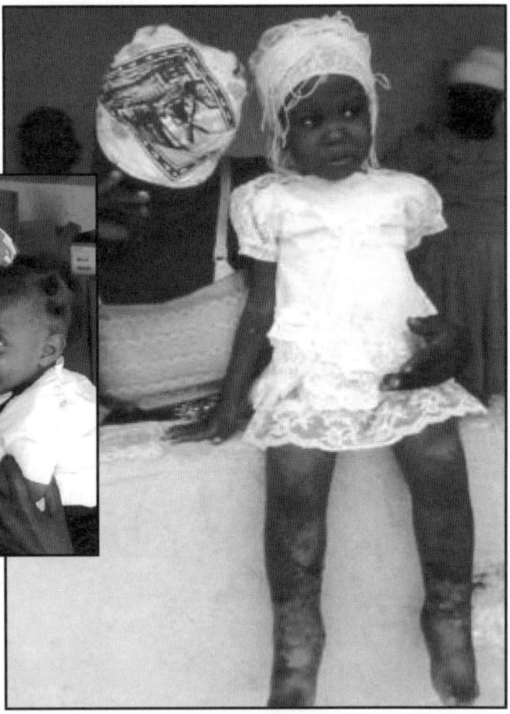

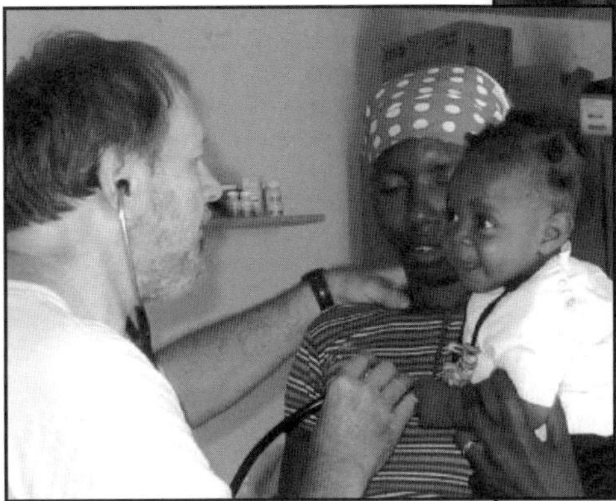

I make decisions—sometimes of the life-or-death variety. So does this mean that I think all my decisions are right? Of course not. But most of my decisions are better than they were six months ago; hopefully, they will be better in six months than they are today.

Somehow, in all of this, God has given me peace. He doesn't give me the diagnosis and prescribe the treatment for me, but he does confirm that I am serving him where I should be, where there are people in need of what I can give. Through these many years in Haiti, I've learned to try to listen and feel for his guidance, to stop and study when I come up against something that is way out of my ball park, and simply to respond in as safe a way as he gives me the knowledge.

So, what came of my young patient? He walked into my next clinic still having some pain, but certainly much better than he had been three days earlier. I treated him further and he seems to be on his way to a normal life now. And the two babies? I haven't seen them since that day, but I expect they'll return to the clinic within a couple of weeks. Hopefully their mothers are following our instructions and they too are on the long road to recovery.

An unnamed missionary cries out from the siege.

WADING WITH GOD

It's been a very tough week. My husband and I can testify that the devil has been hard at work. Although we each are struggling for different reasons, our situations are intertwined. Hence, our individual struggles are exacerbating one another.

This week I've been dealing with a lot of uncertainty regarding the upcoming birth of our child. Part of my emotional response is definitely related to a lack of good sleep, a busy schedule, and hormones. But doubt and concern also have entered my mind as the pressure mounts to decide where to give birth. I've even had some nightmares. (This is something rather new for me because I am not, by nature, a fearful person.) Part of the confusion is that there are positives and negatives to each possible choice—giving birth at home or in a hospital one and a half hours away.

When I was pregnant last time, I heard a clear message from God promising safety in giving birth in our home. I've been begging for direction and the same sense of peace this time, but this has eluded me. I've also been overcome with feelings of guilt as I wrestle with being excited about this new baby, who wasn't planned. I've cried many tears this week.

Wading with God through unknown waters

Today, after a long talk with a good friend, I was in the car. As our son controlled the MP3 player, a song came on that forcefully grabbed my attention. I asked him to play it again because the words were meant just for me. The singer pointed at evidences of God's intervention in her life before, but she was struggling again because what she was facing seemed so much more serious this time. Would God help again? Would he be there for me? She made the decision to let go and trust him, even through the uncertainty. The song made me think of a person hanging on a cliff edge just by one hand. Should she let go and fling herself off into God's arms? Would God really catch her?

As I listened to the song, my tears were unstoppable as God reminded me of thoughts I'd had about the Israelites a few weeks ago. I'd been amazed that they couldn't trust him after all the ways they'd seen him work. And now here I was acting the very same way. God reminded me that he's always been with me and protected me; I have nothing to fear. So why do I doubt?

God reminded me that he's always been with me and protected me; I have nothing to fear.

But I'm not the only one struggling in our home. My husband is facing intense challenges too. He has had continuous struggles with the administration. It is very difficult when his opinions are disregarded in his areas of expertise, particularly when he feels that safety is affected. Changes have been made that require him to answer directly to a very difficult person. This has been a cause of continual stress and frustration. Oh, how we need wisdom! Above all, we pray for patience, that God might be glorified in the midst of all these challenges.

As I write, my heart is heavy. We don't know what all of this confusion means. We love this country and the people here. We know that God has a perfect plan for our family, even if we don't see or understand it. We want to be faithful to him whether all of this is a chain of events set in motion to bring about change in our lives or whether this is a test to stand firm through an attack of the enemy. We pray for perseverance and peace and to trust God and rely completely on his direction as we wade through these churning waters with him.

How God is growing his church in a land where Christians are persecuted.

Holy Washing

Worship and tea go together.

"Holy washing." That's what we call baptism in our part of the world where more than 99 percent of the population is Muslim and Christians are often persecuted for their faith.

In February 2009, we experienced God's grace in a wonderful way when "Olive" obeyed the Lord Jesus in baptism. Trying to keep our profile as close to local culture as possible, we meet for worship in comfortable living rooms where we drink tea and sit around together as friends.

But baptism presents a bit of a challenge during the winter when cold weather prohibits a visit to the seaside. The women resolved this issue by going into the bathroom and dousing Olive in buckets of water. Since they are not allowed to see a woman in an immodest situation, the men respectfully waited in another room according to their culture.

Immediately after the baptism, another observer, "Susan," arrived at the apartment. After leaving her sixth husband, she had moved in with her brother Ray. Although both Ray and Susan had witnessed baptisms before, Susan reacted to Olive's baptism with an explosion of anger and fear, threatening to bring the police and the press. Olive patiently listened to Susan and very calmly explained, "This was my decision and my faith. I wanted to be baptized." Praise God! Only minutes after her baptism, Olive had stood firm against persecution in her own home.

Only two months later, we were privileged to share in another "holy washing" on a wonderful Sunday when fifteen friends (including children) celebrated the resurrection of Jesus together. Of these folks, two were Bible correspondence course (BCC) contacts we have known for some years. They traveled a long distance from their homes to join the celebration and be baptized. Three of the other guests were BCC contacts from our neighborhood. One of them brought his entire family with two teenage children and a co-worker friend.

Only minutes after her baptism, Olive stood firm against persecution in her own home.

After a worship service and a picnic at a nearby tea garden, we relocated to our home for the baptism of the two men from out of town. All the men in the gathering crowded into our bathroom to witness their baptism. As one stepped into the water, he remarked, "I'm really so happy about finally getting to do this!" He knelt down in the filled bathtub while I poured copious amounts of water over him, declaring, "You enter the water a dead man; you come out resurrected with Jesus." As he emerged laughing, he announced to all, "I'm coming out a new man!"

After baptizing the men, I told the women who'd gathered in the kitchen that the water was still warm in case anyone else wanted to be baptized. We all felt surprise when the wife of the newest BCC contact stood up and said firmly that she was willing. Following some discussion and answering questions, the ladies prepared for her baptism. The men waited in another room while her family and the ladies witnessed her baptism in the tub. Her 16-year-old daughter seemed especially moved and visibly showed tears as she watched her mother go through the sober act of being buried and rising with Christ.

When we rejoined the men, her husband—who says he isn't quite ready to be baptized yet—stood up and gave her a big hug, affirming her decision. She was the seventh Muslim we have baptized in the past year and a half, all of whom we have come to know through the Bible correspondence course.

We ended the amazing and surprising day with prayers for the sick and those with employment problems. Our house, which is always a bit crowded with a family of seven, was packed with children of all ages and adults from various walks of life, giving us a deep sense of pleasure seeing the Lord plant the foundation of not just one but two new churches, one here in our part of the city and the other in an otherwise unreached area further away.

For the past two years, hundreds of believers around the world have engaged in P50K ("Pray 50,000" new believers for our country). The current total is 2,000 baptized. Praise the Lord that in April 2009 another three were added! To be part of this harvest is a wonderful privilege for us. God heard our prayers and is answering, although often in ways completely unexpected. May many hundreds more soon come into the reign of Jesus Christ is our prayer.

Cityscape in the land of "holy washing"

Exhausted, I longed to be restored…

In the Palm of His Hand

by Andrei Kolegov
(Chelyabinsk, Russia)

I'd always wondered what it was like to experience the hand of the Lord. The thought that God desires such intimacy with us to want to stretch out his hand and envelop his children in loving care has always had special significance to me. After all, Jesus used his hands not only to carve wood but also to touch the sick, comfort the despairing, and serve the bread and the wine. All these involved using his hands. Even on the cross, his hands were pierced for our sins.

In the summer of 2008, a church group of 100 people, mostly youth, was heading to summer camp in the Ural Mountains. What I desired most was to rest in the palm of God's hand. After a month of meetings and extensive traveling, including hours in the air, I wanted to rest more than anything—but youth camps are not quite the place for that. Living in a tent far from civilization with 100 youth running around does not exactly promote restoration. I discovered that maybe it does.

The place chosen for the camp was perfect. Located about two miles from a village, it was quaint, peaceful, and surrounded by hills. A river cut through the middle of the tiny valley where the campsite was located. The campsite alone spelled out the Lord's presence. And then the Lord sent us perfect weather—sunny and hot—complemented with beautiful sunsets, gorgeous flowers, and solemn pine trees, all announcing joyfully, "God is the creator of all."

The staff had prepared well for our arrival. Tents had been erected, kitchen equipment installed, and the program readied. Everybody was eager for camp to begin. Each year there are first timers who come, some of whom make decisions to open their hearts to Jesus. Every year many grow spiritually and are blessed richly by God. And every year some want to be baptized during camp. Seeing God touching, healing, and changing people is what I enjoy best in ministry. Summer youth camp is ideal for that: you see it all compressed into a short time.

Typically, small problems of some kind arise with such a group of mixed friends and newcomers: a conflict, somebody not feeling well or getting too tired, rain, or something else. Surprisingly, that summer's camp was trouble free. Eleven people received Christ as Savior, four were baptized, and the program ran without a hitch. As a result, everybody had a good deal of fun, and we all grew in our understanding of who God is and what his plans for our lives are.

Landscape of tents nestled between mountain ranges (above); Andrei baptizing two teenage campers (right)

Halfway through the camp as I was looking around one day, I was struck when I counted the hills surrounding our campsite. There were five of them—like fingers on your hand. The valley was protected from all winds, and we felt shielded from any problems because the Lord's presence was so evident around us. Suddenly I realized that I was being held in the palm of God's hand. It was what I'd longed for. Basking in the sunshine, I could only thank God for letting me experience this along with his restoration and blessings.

The summer is gone. But whether we feel it or not, God's presence never departs from us. Do you feel in the palm of his hand? If not, it is only a prayer away. No need to travel to Siberia and wait for the summer. No need to wait for eternity or anything else. The only need is to seek God's face and to love and trust him under all circumstances. I pray his hand will touch and bless you, no matter where you are on the globe, as you walk with him daily.

No stranger to adversity, she proves…

YOU DON'T HAVE TO BE AN EAGLE TO SOAR

by Kathy Simpson
(Plovdiv, Bulgaria)

Tsonka coordinates the orphanage ministry for the Plovdiv congregation. Recently we shared the back seat of the van as the church group returned from the children's home. She showed me photographs from the technology education conference she attended in Malta during the summer. She'd worked hard the past 12 months to earn a certificate in this field and had made a good choice. Indeed, there weren't enough students choosing French this year, and she was notified that her contract as a language teacher wouldn't be renewed. She does, however, have a position teaching computer science.

It's obvious that Tsonka has gained further skills. She put them to good use in a computerized presentation projected for the orphanage kids. During the ride home, she used her laptop to show me some techniques she'd learned. The European Union's Education Department sponsored the event. Teachers across the EU requested grants for this continuing education experience, and she was one of 25 accepted for the four-day seminar.

The participants were from many nations, including France, Italy, Finland, Poland, and, of course, Bulgaria. All official instruction and workgroup interchange was in English. That amazes me, but it is one more confirmation of the expanding use of English as a common language. Tsonka was amazed by something else.

She marveled that everything ran so smoothly. There was a printed schedule, and it was followed just as it was printed. The materials were in perfect order, and all participants received identical notebooks. Each morning and afternoon, the conference provided beverages and snacks for breaks. At midday, everyone was given a box lunch and directions to nearby parks. In the evenings, the group enjoyed excursions to tourist sites. Each person received a 2-gig pen drive from a technology company, and they were all identical! Tsonka was overwhelmed by the seminar's organization.

Even though we've been in Bulgaria for four years, I was surprised by her reaction to what seemed completely normal to me. It was, after all, an international conference. Why would you expect anything less?

Tsonka's perspective, I realize, is one of a teacher who has worked for almost 20 years in a system that doesn't print a calendar for the school year. The beginning date is routine: on or near September 15. Other details seem to be filled in as the year progresses. For instance, no one seems to know exactly when Christmas break begins until a day or two before. Last year after the normal succession of six national holidays in May, officials decided too many days had been missed and scheduled school on two consecutive Saturdays. Facilities and materials are improving but still lag behind Western standards.

All in all, Tsonka's reaction is an indication of how far Bulgaria is behind other EU nations. But her attendance at this conference also indicates the progress being made. It is certainly a sign of Tsonka's personal achievement, although it isn't the first time she has risen above the fray. She's faced adversity and persevered many times in her life.

She tells of sitting beneath the table in her grandparents' crowded apartment. Believers gathered there regularly for Bible study and prayer. The fear of being reported by a disgruntled neighbor, the dread of retribution by the Communist government for their illegal gatherings always heightened the emotional atmosphere in the room. Tsonka especially remembers the people kneeling in prayer, tears streaming down their cheeks as they lifted fervent petitions to the Lord. Their faith made a lasting impression on the young child. She learned that belief requires commitment, a willingness to pay the price.

As a twelve-year-old, she made an incredibly bold statement against the Soviet system. As the entire school prepared for the annual May Day celebration, the children practiced a song praising the glorious Communist state. Tsonka decided she could not and would not participate. Several times she asked to be excused from the choir, but permission was

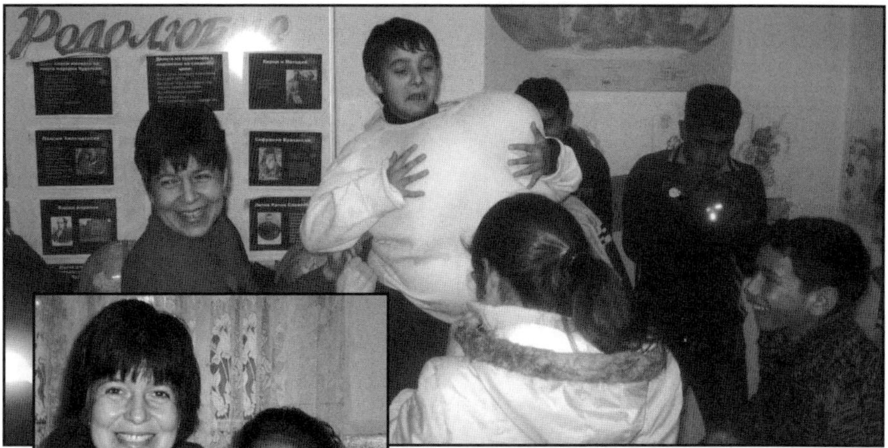

Tsonka playing with orphanage children (above) and sharing special moments with one teenage resident (left)

denied. When the day arrived, the audience focused its attention on the choir of children. Like all the other girls, Tsonka wore a white blouse and a big bow in her hair. She blended in with the crowd until the music began; then she astonished everyone by turning her back to the conductor and the crowd. The song went on but it was clear that Tsonka did not agree with its message.

Fortunately, her parents didn't suffer any consequence for her behavior, but Tsonka did. A "bad character" mark followed her throughout her school years. The high school French teacher, who later became her career mentor, personal friend, and prayer partner, told Tsonka that in all her years of teaching she'd never had another student whose record contained such a scathing assessment of character and deportment. Only by being an exceptional student had she overcome the disrepute of being a dissenter.

Tsonka has faced opposition not only for her political views but also for her faith choices. Her in-laws, who are Orthodox in tradition, attacked her for her membership in the Bulgarian Evangelical Church of God. They irrationally blame her for their son's death. It was the very faith they abhorred that sustained her during her husband's illness and final days.

This year Tsonka faced another family crisis—the likely loss of her job. But she moved from being a widow with two teenaged daughters to support and little prospect for employment, to someone who completed a course of study, attended an international conference, and received a contract to teach a new subject. We say, "Bravo, Tsonka, and slava na Boga (praise to God)!" This has been a difficult and exhausting year, but she has continued to trust the Lord, remembering, "Those who hope in the Lord will renew their strength. They will soar on wings like eagles; they will run and not grow weary, they will walk and not be faint" (Isaiah 40:31).

We'll continue to pray with Tsonka. We expect her to soar.

The Trek

by Jon Lambert (Ecuador)

Bella Vista de las Mines is a rural congregation that basically was abandoned when its founding mission turned most of its Ecuadorian work over to national leadership that did not have the resources to continue rural works.

Seeking to learn more about the Bible, teenage converts from Bella Vista began attending our Bible Institute in 2002. As the years passed, up to seven Bella Vista students at a time attended. In December 2007, Pastor Antonio attended our national committee meeting and asked to begin the process to enter the Church of God. He noted that because of the institute, all the church's young people had become Church of God and had returned from the institute and taught the elders. "All that remains," he said, "is to change the sign."

Recently, Pastor Antonio told of a man who'd trekked over four hours from deep in the rain forest to the church because he'd heard they could show him how to meet God. Moved by the story, I remembered something Oswald J. Smith said, "No one has the right to hear the gospel twice while there remains someone who has not heard it once."

They prayed for a sign to know the truth.

Chocolate Jesus

by Rhonda Philips
(Berlin, Germany)

My memories of Easter as a small girl are filled with egg hunts and grass-filled baskets brimming with colorful eggs, chocolates, and a chocolate bunny. But for Easter 2009, I received an unexpected gift when I traveled with my family to visit one of our regional coworkers. There, on Good Friday, I learned about a chocolate Jesus from Turna. (I will call her this because using her real name could endanger her life.)

Turna grew up in a Muslim home and remembers two things in particular: they were poor and her mother was severely depressed. At the age of 12, Turna watched as the depression grew into thoughts of suicide. Finally, her mother decided to kill herself. But first, she would visit a neighborhood Christian church. On her first and second attempts to enter, the building was locked. But the third time, a volunteer janitor heard the knock and unlocked the door. Seeing her desperation, he prayed with her and gave her a New Testament. Turna's mother took it home and

Kelley, Rhonda, and Christian Philips

hid it because she felt she must investigate this faith before exposing her children to it.

"We knew where Mama hid stuff and found the Bible in the back of the cold oven," Turna told me, adding that she and her two sisters retrieved it and read it under their covers by flashlight. "When we read John 3:16, we were amazed. Could it really be true?"

The three sisters agreed to find out by praying for a sign. Prayer was familiar to them because it is an important part of Islam. But while Turna had prayed many times before, she'd never felt her prayers going beyond the four white walls of their house, and she'd never received an answer. Perhaps she wasn't praying right, or maybe she was doing something else wrong, she thought. Still, praying seemed the right step now.

But what should the sign be? The girls knew that it must be something that had never happened before in their lives. If God really loved them enough to give his son Jesus, then they'd ask him to confirm this through an amazing sign: they asked that their mother bring home three chocolate bars, one for each of them. Of course they'd eaten chocolate before, but only rarely. Even then it would be broken into small pieces and shared among them. So they knew that this would be a miracle, and they waited to see what would happen.

To their amazement, their mother returned with three bars of chocolate, one for each daughter. It was the sign they'd prayed God would show them, and they believed in his son, Jesus Christ, who'd been revealed to them first in the Bible and now in chocolate.

Around this same time, Turna's depressed mother had a dream. Since dreams carry an important meaning in their culture, she told the pastor about it and asked him to interpret its meaning.

"My dream was of a beautiful field of soft green grass. A stream was running through it, and it was filled with peace," she recounted to him.

Responding, he read Psalm 23 to her: "The Lord is my shepherd, I shall not want. He makes me to lie down in green pastures; He leads me beside still waters. He restores my soul…" As her daughters had responded to the sign, Turna's mother now believed in the Good Shepherd.

Today, Turna is 19 years old. She, her mother, and her two sisters are all followers of Jesus in a difficult and hostile environment. Turna works in a bookstore operated by Christians in a very large Muslim city.

Interestingly, the volunteer janitor in the church who gave her mother the New Testament works alongside Turna. Now 15 years old, Turna's sister attends a private school. She left public school after receiving death threats from other students because she is a Christian. But through prayer, she has decided to return to public school so she can share her faith in Jesus there.

"It must have been difficult being a young Christian teenager in a Muslim school," I said to Turna.

Agreeing, she told me how she was forbidden to talk about Jesus during school time and how she was ridiculed by both teachers and students. Still, her friends surrounded her during breaks and asked many questions. She told them she'd answer their questions after school and spent hours talking then about Jesus and the Bible. Naturally, some friends debated with her, trying to persuade her to return to Islam, and this left her feeling alienated.

But she would not turn back. Why? Because she'd been touched deeply by Jesus, the one who answers prayer. Even when her father abandoned the family over their faith and they were desperate for the basic necessities of life, they prayed and Jesus miraculously provided for them over and over again.

Please pray for Turna and her family. Pray also for the safety of Muslims who come to Christ and for the protection of those who risk their very lives to share Christ in this difficult part of the world.

Three chocolate bars, an answer to the prayer of three sisters

A busy missionary meets Cinderella.

Cinderella's Delight

by Kara Goldman
(Chelyabinsk, Russia)

The washing machine in our apartment is very special: it has a name and has become a member of the family. With a family of five, one constant occupation is laundry. This is where Cinderella enters the picture. Our washer is named Cinderella. We did not name her; it is actually the name printed on the front of the machine.

We are very thankful for Cinderella. When the dirty clothes pile up, it has become fun to joke and say, "Cinderella! Time to get busy!" She never complains or is unwilling to work, even if it's a day where multiple loads need washing. Cinderella just scrubs and rinses and spins, turning clothes that were dirty and smelly into ones that are clean and fresh. Then we put them on a drying rack, kind of an indoor clothesline. If I had a dryer, I would call it Prince Charming. But alas, no Prince Charming is available here.

At times, I think my honorary name should be Cinderella. It is a full-time occupation to try to manage the household; keep kids, clothes, and home in a semblance of cleanliness and order; and make sure that food is in the pantry and on the table. Unfortunately, my work does not end there. I am also my children's home-school teacher, a student in a graduate program, and a missionary with ministry responsibilities. Sometimes when I feel overwhelmed, it's nice to make Cinderella do some of the work.

There is also another side of Cinderella that is regularly present in our household. It is the world of princesses, dress-up, and fairytales that our five-year-old daughter likes to visit. Here there are no chores and drudgery, only princes, pretty twirling dresses, and balls. Abigail dances and spins and adores it when we play dress-up together.

I recently came upon the song "Cinderella" and the story behind it, written by Steven Curtis Chapman. The lyrics poignantly implore us not

Doing laundry for the Goldmans requires an indoor drying rack (right) and "Cinderella's delight" (below).

to neglect the precious moments we have to enjoy with the people who matter most because "the clock will strike midnight" and the moment will be gone. What a powerful message. We all know the story of the little girl who was unfairly made a servant but willingly served anyhow. Then one day everything changed. She was invited to a ball, met a young man who turned out to be the prince, and soon left it all behind.

Who is Cinderella? My washer? Me? My daughter? Every little girl? Maybe it is all of us who get so busy, frustrated, and tired. And honestly, we never get done with everything on our must-do lists.

As I've reflected, I realize that my busyness has caused me not to cherish every moment with my children. Sometimes it has even caused me to focus only on getting things done rather than doing them with a willing and glad heart. So, the Cinderellas in my life are teaching me to slow down, to live in the moment, and, most of all, to love my Savior and my family unreservedly. I am learning to take time to spend with my heavenly Father who longs for his Cinderellas to stop, delight in him, and remember that we all have an invitation to his ball. The Prince, our Savior, is waiting!

Latin America's regional coordinator provides an exciting...

Bird's Eye View

by David Miller
(Cochabamba, Bolivia)

Barbara and I decided to take an overland trip from Indiana to Bolivia in the fall of 2009 so that we could visit most of the 20 countries where the Church of God has congregations in Latin America. This vast region spans more than 4,500 miles from north to south and offers many diverse subcultures. Among them, the Church of God is also a widely diverse movement in Latin America. Here is some of what we saw.

The line of white-robed figures stretched from the river up the steep bank. Thirty-two new Christians, most of them older teens and twenty-somethings, would testify that day to their decision to follow Christ by being baptized in the Tapajos River, a tributary of Brazil's great Amazon.

As each candidate was called into the water, a pastor read aloud a verse of Scripture the individual had chosen. The same scripture was custom-printed on his or her baptismal certificate as a reminder of God's promises and the new believer's commitment to the Lord. Hundreds of family members, friends, and invited guests lined the riverbank as witnesses. When it was over, they stayed on for barbecues, water sports, and siestas in hammocks strung among the trees.

The half dozen Church of God congregations in and around Itaituba, Brazil, celebrate baptismal Sunday every year in late September or early October. The line of candidates has been getting longer each year, a testimony to the growth spurt the church in Amazonia (northern Brazil) has been experiencing. Expansion has spawned several new congregations planted in towns and cities up and down river from Itaituba.

What sparked the revival? I asked Oreste Greiner, who with his wife Marlene helped pioneer the Church of God in Amazonia in the 1970s.

He did not have to think about his answer. "Our seminary," he declared. "When young men and women began to answer God's call and prepare themselves for ministry, we began to see a whole new vision of what the church could be in this part of Brazil."

Without doubt, discipleship and leader development are key components in growing the church into the next generation. Amazonia's leaders also laud their historic partnership with North America, beginning in 1974 when Donald Johnson and Maurice Caldwell purchased the first plot of land in Itaituba for a mission base. They did so by faith and because the Trans-Amazon Highway ended there and they knew it would bring hundreds of thousands of new settlers into the region. Today, it seems that their investment—and faith—have paid off.

Cuba has taken an innovative approach to preparing pastoral workers—by necessity. Scarce resources and inadequate transportation make it virtually impossible for those training for ministry to attend classes in a central location. So Regla Pedroso, rector of the School of Biblical Theology, became an itinerant professor. Every three months, the former chemistry teacher tours the island to lecture, collect homework, and give exams.

The Miller family—(from left) Barbara, Molly, Ben, and David—setting off on an overland trip to Latin America

Her students report she is tough but fair. Regla says she is interested in more than just academics. "Being prepared for the ministry does not simply mean having intellectual knowledge," she wrote to me. "It implies a personal and affectionate relationship with God that manifests itself in a lifestyle conformed to his will."

It is a privilege to work alongside dedicated servants who labor in God's Latin American vineyard every day.

In 2007, Pedroso enlisted an assistant rector, an academic secretary, and provincial coordinators for each of the school locations. Course offerings geared to pastoral workers' distinctive calling and interests include basic theology, ministerial studies, evangelism, and Christian education. "We are also looking for ways to assist our students to continue their personal growth beyond graduation," she explains.

The Cuban church needs many pastors, evangelists, and Sunday school teachers to shepherd its 89 congregations and house churches. While funding from North America helps support the training centers, purchase educational materials, and cover travel costs for Pedroso and her volunteer staff, she points out these donations supplement the precious offerings of the Cubans themselves.

"We are working with a lot of effort and little economic resources," she reports. "Some of the brothers [here] who have been blessed personally have then contributed their valuable offerings so that we can continue the work."

A trip to Colombia in March 2008 for a leadership training seminar reminded me what amazingly talented and godly leaders—like Regala Pedroso—are working to build the Church of God in Latin America.

Israel and Elizabet Osorio are bivocational pastors in Bogotá's Marly district. To earn their living, Israel teaches at two universities and two theological seminaries. Meanwhile, Elizabet, who leads praise and worship at the Marly church, is completing her master's degree in biblical sciences with a view to joining her husband one day as a professor.

Angel and Jeaneth Pinto have pastored a thriving congregation in Puerto Asis for 20 years despite intense dangers from guerrilla groups and drug traffickers. They conduct two programs for needy children and broadcast the gospel over three church-owned radio stations. Angel wrote me after launching yet another new church, this one in Popayán: "I am sensing God's call to plant churches and radio stations, and to prepare leaders for the glory of God."

José Antonio and Marta Jimenez became leaders of Bogotá's Catalina congregation in 2002. José works full-time with the Colombia Bible Society, distributing Scriptures and training other pastors in Bible-study techniques. Marta resigned from public school teaching to dedicate more time to training Sunday school teachers and children's workers. The Jimenez family plans eventually to transform the three-story building where their congregation worships into a full-time training center for church leaders.

On a visit to Peru, I spent time with Nicolás and Telvi Pérez and the Chepén church, the largest Church of God congregation in that country. Nicolás gave me a tour of the lovely D. S. Warner School next door,

Cochabamba, Bolivia, the end of the road trip (left); Dave Miller and Regala Pedroso, of Cuba's School of Biblical Theology (below)

which was primed and ready to start a new school term the following day. The Chepén church hosted the International Forum for Kingdom Workers in August 2008. As part of that event, they also planned a workshop for local educators and parents on playing a more effective role in educating Peru's youth.

Jonas and Neidy Tello plant churches in and around Iquitos, a city in Peru's torrid eastern jungles. Like most pastors and evangelists in Latin America, the couple lives on modest means and uses all resources at hand and every possible opportunity to build the church. In a recent e-mail, Jonas shared:

> [Soon] we will be dedicating our [new] temple, and then we will visit congregations [in other areas]. Thank God for new church plants in Yurimaguas and Tarapoto. My father, Anselmo Tello Morales, pastor of our church in Caja de Agua, Lima, visited us for one month. On his way home, he passed through Yurimaguas. There he met some brothers who told him that years ago someone had given them *La Trompeta* magazines. They also mentioned they had adopted the name 'Church of God.' [As they talked, they] realized all they shared the same teachings and doctrine.
>
> My dad was there two weeks and then went on to Tarapoto. He found other brothers there who need to be built up in the faith, and, thanks to God, we now have a new congregation there. Our desire is that the Church of God grows and is strengthened [throughout Peru]."

It excites me to see God use modest resources like *La Trompeta* (and its English ancestor, *The Gospel Trumpet*) to help dedicated servants like these plant churches. North American youth are also playing a part. Recently, they purchased an outboard motor for Jonas Tello through the Spread the Word (STW) program. Now the dugout canoe and its outboard propel Jonas and Neidy to unreached communities along the Amazon and its tributaries.

These leaders represent hundreds of dedicated servants of God who labor in his Latin America vineyard every day, meeting enormous challenges, often with limited material resources. It is a privilege to work alongside them.

God used a birthday party to unite…

TWO GIRLS, TWO COUNTRIES

by Julie Foster and Kathi Sellers
(Indianapolis, Indiana; Anderson, Indiana)

As a mother, I (Julie) have long been concerned that my two children were being sucked blindly into the materialistic culture of the United States, even though we as a family try to live pretty simple lives. My kids are both generous, but they also have serious lists of things they want and believe they need in order to be happy. They have well-off, loving, and generous grandparents, as well as bachelor uncles who seem to try and outdo each other in the gift department at Christmas, Easter, Halloween, and all the other merchandising days Americans celebrate. Some of the most unfortunate episodes of excess have come at birthday parties. Our children are allowed to have guest parties at ages five, ten, thirteen, and sixteen.

As my daughter Elizabeth approached her thirteenth birthday, she planned a sleepover with ten girls. I mentioned that since her parents and

The Herrera-Blanco family—Guillermo, Juanita, Lesly, and Xochilt

grandparents would have some very nice gifts for her, perhaps she would like to think about forgoing the traditional gift party. Liz had already asked for a Mexican-themed fiesta party with a taco bar for supper and a piñata. Building on her idea, I suggested that there might be a missionary in Mexico who could use a small amount of money for a youth-related cause. I told Liz that perhaps each girl could be asked to take the money she intended to spend on a gift and give it to such a concern. I asked Liz to think about it, but I made sure she knew that it was her decision. Yet only a few minutes later, she agreed that it was an excellent idea and entered wholeheartedly into the plan.

We contacted Pastor Broyles from our church (Church at the Crossing in Indianapolis, Indiana) and asked him to help us find a missionary in Central America or Mexico who might be helped by such a gift. We were put in touch with Wayne and Kathi Sellers, then missionaries in Costa Rica, and through them we heard about Xochilt, a teenager in Nicaragua. I shared the information with Liz, and she became even more excited about the birthday party we were planning.

When we made up the invitations, we specified no gifts. Instead, we wrote out information about Xochilt on the back of the invitation. Responding generously, all the girls seemed excited that the money would go to help a young lady like themselves in another country. Afterward, one parent told me that she wanted to suggest that her children do something similar, but she was afraid they would reject the idea. Another man said he was thinking about doing something similar at his child's birthday.

This is only half of the story. Although I was in Costa Rica and not in Indiana at the time, I (Kathi) remember this unusual birthday party well because Elizabeth Foster had really impressed me! It was hard to imagine that a thirteen-year-old wanted her birthday party guests to give money to a mission project in Central America. I became the link between Elizabeth and Xochilt.

At the time, Xochilt was fourteen years old. Her parents, Guillermo Herrera and Juanita Blanco, are national missionaries to Nicaragua. Three years earlier, in 2003, they had moved from Costa Rica to Jinotepe, Nicaragua, to start a Church of God there. Xochilt was not thrilled about moving to Nicaragua; she was happy in Costa Rica, the only home she'd ever known (even though her parents had been born in Nicaragua). But

The Church of God in Jinotepe, Nicaragua (above); Elizabeth Foster (right), whose birthday supported missions

three years can bring a lot of change, and Xochilt adjusted to her new life and began helping her parents with their ministry.

Although Xochilt is a bit shy, she soon found her niche teaching Sunday school. The kids who came adored her, and the Sunday school began to grow. Pretty soon, Xochilt was overseeing two other young teachers. They had few resources—not even Sunday school books to teach from—so they developed their own lessons from the Bible. Xochilt and her teachers were creative, and the kids delighted in class; soon there were 50 eager children attending.

When Xochilt heard about Elizabeth and the $165 she'd collected at her birthday party for the Sunday school, her eyes were wide with surprise and delight. On her next visit to Costa Rica, we accompanied her to buy Sunday school books for teachers and students, a CD of children's music, and little cards that could be used for handcrafts or as small gifts to award the children. God used the generous heart of a thirteen-year-old in the United States to meet the needs of a fourteen-year-old Sunday school teacher and 50 Nicaraguan children in Nicaragua.

Today, Elizabeth is a 15-year-old high school sophomore; Xochilt, her neighbor to the south, is graduating from high school. Although the girls have never met in person, their hearts were brought together across the miles by God's love. Two girls, two countries, but one heart in Jesus Christ, our Lord.

How God shines light and hope…

In a Besieged City

by Abby Smith
(Bogotá, Colombia)

Bogotá: the capital city and heart of Colombia, home to nearly eight million people and a growing urban sprawl, thanks in part to the steady influx of *desplazados,* families who have been displaced by the violence that consumes much of the rest of the country. In a nation raging with civil war, Bogotá is a refuge, a cool mountain fortress that protects *desplazados* from the heat of conflict in the jungles below.

Unfortunately, Bogotá also is home to countless people caught in the cycle of urban poverty: parents who cannot provide for their children, children abandoned by their families, teenagers turning to drugs or violence to escape their pain, and so many more. I had the privilege to spend eleven weeks in Bogotá in the summer of 2008 during an internship that changed my life and set me on course to return to this besieged city.

For my internship, I worked with both Church of God congregations and some Mennonite programs. I fell in love with the people from the Church of God, but the Mennonite work also intrigued me because it put me into direct contact with many people who had known and experienced violence firsthand.

During my stay, the Colombian government rescued fifteen high-profile hostages in a covert operation that stunned and delighted the world. While the nation rejoiced, I found mixed reactions among the *desplazados.* Some felt that shifting the national focus toward the problem of kidnapping took away from the plight of the internally displaced. After hearing one man complain, I remember thinking, "It's just that there are so many problems here, no one can focus on all of them at once. If we talk about the hostages, we forget the *desplazados.* If we focus on them, we forget the urban poor…" Rejoicing turned to heaviness as my heart weighed the magnitude of problems that the Colombian people continued to face.

Even in the midst of despair, there is hope in this city besieged by violence and fear. During my visit I heard story after countless story of those who found their hope in the Prince of Peace. A man I'll call Arturo worked as a volunteer with a local feeding program. His family had fallen into disfavor with one of the armed groups when he was a teenager, and as an adult, Arturo and his wife (I'll call her Helena) found themselves displaced in Bogotá. They sought help from a local Protestant church that not only provided for their physical needs but also introduced them to Jesus Christ. Because getting a job could leave a paper trail and reveal Arturo's location, the church next offered him the chance to work as a volunteer in their feeding program. In exchange, they would provide a rented home in the neighborhood.

Anyone who meets Arturo would never imagine that his family has such a sad history; the joy and hope he has in Jesus Christ radiates from the smile on his face. When Helena had the opportunity to get a job and bring in some extra income for the family, she took it immediately, only to learn days later that it was a scam. Although participating in the con likely would have provided some much-needed funds, she knew as a Christian that she couldn't cheat people. She quit her job and began to search for a more honest living. Although they continue to face difficult

A shanty town in Costa Rica, similar to where Abby Smith will work in Colombia

Abby Smith and the family she leaves behind to answer God's call to Colombia

circumstances, Arturo and Helena are shining examples of the hope of Jesus Christ in the midst of a city besieged in darkness and fear.

Stories of hope abound in the Church of God as well. Israel, a professor and a staunch Marxist atheist, came to the church more than two decades ago, hoping to find out more information about the "myth" many of his students believed. He developed a friendship with Mendoza Taylor, a missionary from Panama who had founded the church, and Mendoza ultimately led Israel to a relationship with God. Israel feels that his primary calling is to be a professor, and his repertoire of classes now includes philosophy, New Testament, and Greek.

For the past thirteen years, Israel has also served as the pastor of one of the Church of God congregations. In this war-torn nation where political ideologies lead to so much violence, winning the battle for the mind is critical. Pastor Israel Osorio serves as a living example of how the power of God's love, demonstrated through God's people, can free even the most imprisoned hearts and minds from the chains of darkness and confusion that bind them. Now the families that come to this church to find food for their bodies and spirits also find hope, encouragement, and love in this gentle man of God.

Arturo, Helena, and Israel are just three of many people whose lives testify to the hope of Jesus Christ in a country that has seen decades of tragedy, hopelessness, and turmoil. After weeks of hearing stories of both trials and of triumph, I knew in the summer of 2008 that the Lord was calling me back to Colombia to be a part of the future he has in store for the people of Bogotá. I look forward to learning from these three and others about the true nature of peace. I cannot wait to hear all the testimonies from stories past and stories yet to unfold as the Lord continues to shine hope into this besieged city that I have come to love and call home.

A once-feared gang member and the…

OUTBREAK IN OFELIA

by Jon Lambert
(Quito, Ecuador)

A rented garage was an unlikely place to begin a new church. But the location did nothing to dampen the enthusiasm of Pastor Milton and his wife Lilly. By the end of November 2007, they had labored for three years in the barrio of Ofelia in Quito and had long since outgrown the garage in an amazing growth spurt the likes of which I've never seen before.

Milton's own story is nothing short of dramatic. The former member of one of Ecuador's most dangerous gangs, the pastor first met God in Eloy Alfaro Prison, the top-security penitentiary where the worst criminals in the country are incarcerated. Today Milton continues to spend time there, not as a prisoner but as pastor of the prison

A lively worship celebration of Ophelia Church's second anniversary in 2006

church. In Ofelia, Milton and Lilly faithfully helped the congregation grow into a fellowship of about 50 adults and 20 children. But they were far from satisfied.

Earlier that summer, the Ofelia congregation realized that many unchurched people were uncomfortable attending services in a church building, even one that had begun in a garage. So the congregation began five week-night cell groups in homes. Suddenly, the church's plateau attendance was a thing of the past as people living in nearby neighborhoods surrounding the church began turning up for the home Bible studies and eventually for church services.

> ***In a two-room building, Ophelia Church nearly doubled itself twice in one year!***

Shortly into the growth spurt, Karen and I were present in the Ofelia Church service where five deaf members of an Afro-Ecuadorian family accepted Christ. The joy on their faces was radiant. As we greeted them afterwards, welcoming them into the family of God, they could only respond with muffled cries and groans. But the unintelligible sounds were happy and joyful. The family, shunned by neighbors, had been invited to the cell group of Sister Maria Inez, who related that she didn't know what to do with them after they actually arrived.

"We barely communicated, but they kept returning," she recalls, adding, "They only understood bits and pieces, and none of us knew sign language. But they kept coming because we loved and welcomed them."

This scenario has been repeated in all five cell groups. On November 18, 2007, we were at Ofelia for their third anniversary. Nearly 200 people packed into the sanctuary. By then, Ofelia was renting a two-room building, which they'd converted into a sanctuary. With permission of the owner, they'd also been able to expand one room out to the street in order to accommodate the crowds. So with a 40-foot by 60-foot sanctuary, a one-seat bathroom, a 7-foot- by 9-foot-kitchen and Sunday school room, the Ofelia church had nearly doubled itself twice in one year!

Bursting at the seams, the Ophelia building cannot accommodate the growth of revival.

As the year 2009 began, the outbreak of Holy Spirit activity and neighborhood revival through the Ofelia Church was continuing. The congregation is now actively seeking a bigger building to rent because, after two expansions at their present location, they can no longer seat those coming to services. They are also desperately in need of Sunday school rooms. The short term plan is to begin having two services on Sunday morning rather than to turn people away.

As for the deaf family—among the earliest new believers as the outbreak began—they continue to integrate into the life of the church. I am amazed at the growth of their communication skills. Their shy, stay-in-the-background manner has grown into a more mature confidence in their newfound faith. While before they always sat at the back of the sanctuary, now they eagerly find seats at the front where they can more easily watch the lips of those leading worship or preaching.

Brother Milton is a good pastor who loves and cares for his congregation. Fellow missionary Greg Robertson and I recently began teaching a series of doctrinal classes on Wednesday evenings at the Ofelia Church. But the first thirty minutes of every midweek service is devoted to Brother Milton as he leads a passionate prayer for those in the church and then for the work of God in the world.

I was always amazed and wondered at the miraculous growth of the New Testament church after the Holy Spirit arrived on Pentecost. I wonder no more. I am seeing it here in Ecuador, in a downtrodden neighborhood in Quito. We pray the outbreak will never stop.

After meningitis, he lived in a world of silence.

Last Word, First Word

by Julie Kurrle
(Obligado, Itapua, Paraguay)

"Mama." It was the only word 18-month-old Jorge could say. Then a severe case of meningitis almost took his life. Although the baby survived, he lost his ability to hear. For almost eleven years Jorge lived in silence, the one word he could utter before meningitis fading into a distant memory.

That is, until today. This is the day Jorge and his entire family will remember as the day the silence lifted, thanks to a hearing aid and the hand of God at work through his people. Here's the rest of the story.

It's awesome how God uses many people to bless and touch one life. I first met Jorge five years ago when I visited his rural home and saw how he and his very poor family were struggling financially. One of the Children of Promise sponsored children in Paraguay, Jorge was both intelligent and handsome. He looked normal in every respect, but he was a prisoner of silence. Somehow, I felt like God would help him to hear again, but I didn't have the resources or the contacts to make it happen. God took care of that.

Two years later, a work camp from First Church of God in St. Joseph, Michigan, came to build a new church building where Jorge and his family worshiped. After meeting Jorge, a skilled contractor on the team mentioned that he once had built the office for an audiologist. Hmm, that's good to know, I thought as I filed this new piece of information in my mental storage cabinet.

Then last year, another family from the same church decided they wanted to bless Paraguayan children. So instead of receiving gifts for his fortieth birthday, the father (or husband) asked friends to give to Children of Promise in Paraguay. Amazingly, we received over $1,000! Since Jorge had never received a diagnosis in his infancy—his family simply

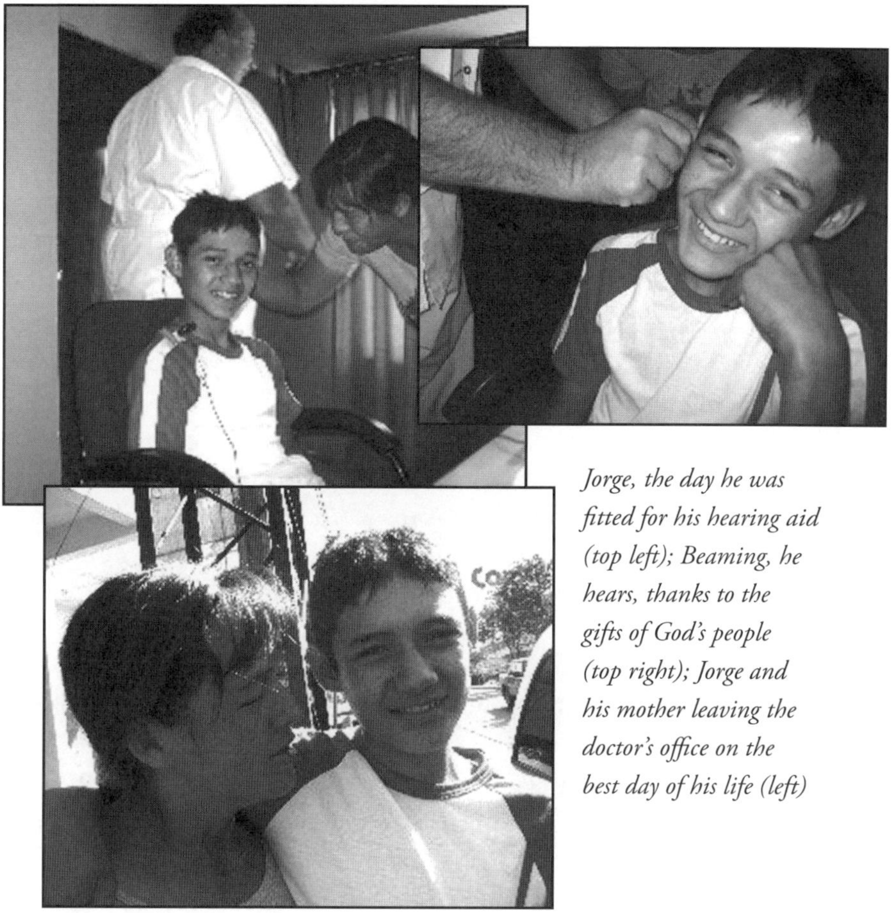

Jorge, the day he was fitted for his hearing aid (top left); Beaming, he hears, thanks to the gifts of God's people (top right); Jorge and his mother leaving the doctor's office on the best day of his life (left)

couldn't afford it—we used the special donation money to get him tested in Encarnación, an hour away. But we drove home in total silence after the audiologist announced the results of the testing: Jorge had 100 percent hearing loss.

"Lord, I just don't understand," I prayed in my heart, disappointment my most evident emotion. "You provided the funds for Jorge's hearing tests, but now it seems even that won't help."

There was one small glimmer of hope remaining. The audiologist suggested we visit a different doctor in town who had better equipment. But when the second doctor tested Jorge's left ear, only a flat line appeared on the monitor. Seeing this, his mother realized there was no hearing capacity there and had to leave the room because she could not stop crying from disappointment.

But God wasn't finished yet. When the audiologist put the machine to Jorge's right ear, Jorge started nodding his head with excitement. He could hear!

"Come inside, come inside!" I called to his mother who was still outside trying to compose herself. "Jorge can hear! He's responding to the machine!"

All in all, we made four different trips to Encarnación. After experiencing a roller coaster of emotions—anxiety, disappointment, and immense joy—we were told that Jorge would benefit from a hearing aid after all. But the joy was short-lived when we learned that a hearing aid would cost more than the family's entire annual income.

Yet I had new hope in my heart as the Lord reminded me of our contractor friend's comment about the audiologist whose office he'd built. Our friend gladly got in touch with that doctor, and she immediately agreed to donate a hearing aid for Jorge. It was valued at over $1,100! Three weeks later I received the hearing aid in the mail, but my heart sank when I saw that the box was completely open. Our mail had been opened on three previous occasions, and every time, whatever was sent to us had been stolen. Yet unbelievably, Jorge's hearing aid was still in the package. God had protected it! Needless to say, we were on our way back to Encarnación nearly immediately.

Because of the power of God's people coming together from different places to do God's bidding with their different gifts, Jorge today can hear. His family and friends have been impacted by the knowledge that complete strangers gave such gifts to them just because of Jesus' love. It brought tears to my eyes to see their responses to this knowledge. I couldn't stop thinking of Paul's words in Romans 10:17, "Faith comes through hearing." Although he was talking about spiritual hearing, I don't believe that's too far off for this young lad who experienced such great love and blessing from people who barely know him. I told him that God gave him new ears because he loves him so much and cares for his life.

By the way, after Jorge was fitted for the hearing aid, he uttered the word "Mama" once again. It had been his last word. Today it was his first.

The shock of melanoma was staggering, but God was there.

The Scar

by Colleen Stevenson
(Kampala, Uganda)

During 1996, our family was on home assignment in the United States and Canada. Those seven months were very busy, and we had a hard time squeezing in all the dental and medical check-ups and various appointments necessary. Sometimes when time is pressing, one can overlook important check-ups. I praise God because he helped us when we might have done just that.

We had two and a half months left before we were to return to Uganda. Because of strikes and medical politics, we had been finding it difficult to see a doctor in Ontario. Finally, a family member gave us a

The Stevenson family: (from left) Logan, Natasha, Tim, Colleen, Tiffany, and Jesse

number for the Missionary Health Institute in Toronto. I phoned and made arrangements for the family to get immunizations and complete physicals, and in December all six of us went in and began the process. We were in good hands.

After my husband Tim and I were checked, the doctor advised us to see a dermatologist because he'd found some sun spots and strangely colored moles. He referred us to one in the town where we were staying. With less than two months of home assignment remaining, Tim went in for his check-up, and finally my turn came. Two areas on my stomach and back were carefully removed for examination. To my surprise, a malignant melanoma spot was found on my lower back. Quickly and efficiently, the doctors had me come in for blood tests, ultra-sounds, and x-rays to see if and how far the melanoma had spread.

Then the waiting began. We waited for test results and for news of—we knew not what! We only knew that God was very close to us, definitely in our midst and helping us in the difficult waiting process.

The doctor then made arrangements for me to be admitted to the hospital, where a very large piece of tissue and muscle was removed to make sure all the cancerous tissue was excised. The shock of having melanoma was staggering. It seemed like a bad dream that was only getting worse as Tim and I talked it through and came to understand the seriousness of my situation. But without doubt, God was there for us and with us, giving us the strength to survive the ordeal. We praised God when the final results showed all the cancer had been removed successfully.

I thank God because the spot was discovered before we returned to Africa. The doctor told me that if I had returned to Uganda for another term, the melanoma surely would have spread throughout my body and it would have been too late to do much about it then.

I now have a scar—a reminder of what happened and of my need for annual check-ups to make sure no new spots appear or change. But the scar is not a morbid blemish. Instead, it reminds me that every little detail of my life is in the Lord's hands and that he is great enough to fill all my needs and to strengthen me in any difficult situation.

UPDATE

Twelve years after Colleen Stevenson shared her cancer story in *No Other Rock* (1998), she wrote this update:

Colleen officiates at a Ugandan wedding

Since the removal of the melanoma, I've been checking regularly for any recurrence. During the first two years, I had to check in every three to six months. Thankfully, the Church of God in Germany arranged for my medical care. I praise God that I've not had any more melanomas since, so we've been able to see God working in many ways.

God has expanded our outreach into Rwanda, Congo, and Sudan. We've been blessed to see changed lives, children cared for through three different sponsorship programs, and women develop through various projects. We've also involved with over 120 schools in Uganda and some in neighboring countries. TAPP was started—a ministry of AIDS prevention. We now reach over 40 centers that serve over 3,000 clients. Jjaja Njagala is helping aged and needy grandmothers have homes for their grandchildren and families. And there is more. We're happy that God spared my life for us to minister to vulnerable communities.

I still have many dreams—starting a radio/recording studio, opening a farm for needy slum kids to visit, and opening up more sponsorship programs in new countries like Burundi. We know that with God all things are possible.

During this time, our four beautiful children have all nearly grown; one of them made me a grandmother in 2008.

For sure, my time on earth was extended for a reason. Some people say I am too ambitious, but I have explained that there is a clock ticking and I want to make good use of God's time.

The signs of God's presence are unmistakable. They are seen in...

The Fingerprints of God

AFRICA

Kirk Bookout

Sometimes when I work with people, it's better than great. Sometimes I wish that everyone in the Church of God could have these amazing experiences.

Many of the people I meet are remarkable, and I am often shocked into wonder. This week it happened again. I listened to "Betty" cry when I spoke with her on the telephone a few days ago. I have been in her home and heard her declare how God has blessed her life and how she feels compelled to do something for him in return.

Life has not been easy for her. She has health issues and has lived alone for decades. Though she has known pain, she is not at all angry or bitter—she is blessed. Betty has been talking with me about a well for Africa. She has read how many people there have no safe water supply. She knows that as women and children walk great distances to retrieve water, they are in danger from predators. She knows that rape along the road to the well is not uncommon. She has questions.

We confirmed that the well would be placed where it was really needed, and that it would be in a safe location for children and women. But it will cost about $ 5,000. Was that too much?

"What now?" Betty asked me. I told her that it was up to her and asked what she wanted to do. Without a pause, she replied, "I'll write a check and mail it today to pay for the well. If there is extra expense, let me know and I'll pay that too."

I told Betty I was blessed because I had the honor of thanking her on behalf of people she will never meet and who may never know her name. The line was silent; Betty was crying. When she could finally speak, she said, "I cannot believe that someone like me can really make a difference. I am so blessed that I get to do this."

Betty tells me she is the blessed one. The one well she has donated will help hundreds, perhaps thousands of people. Yet Betty tells me she is blessed because she can do this. The Lord speaks to me in my amazement, "Be still. Remove your sandals, for you are on holy ground."

—Kirk Bookout
Anderson, Indiana

BELIZE

"Hermano Alfonso!" It was Pastor Juan calling out to us at the open market in our town where he sells his produce every Saturday. He shared the progress of his church and asked for prayer for his family and his need of a reliable vehicle to carry his produce every Friday night to the market in San Ignacio. The dedication and commitment of bivocational pastors in Belize never ceases to amaze us. They hold "regular" full-time jobs to support their full-time pastoral and evangelistic ministries.

Every morning, Pastor Raul wakes up at 3:00 AM to help in the family business, preparing food ingredients to be taken from the town of Orange Walk to Belize City, two hours away. There his oldest son attends a small food stand and Pastor Raul shepherds the church, one of the largest congregations with which we cooperate. He also pastors the Guinea Grass Church. His love for God and joy are remarkable.

One of the most enthusiastic, energetic pastors we know is Pastor Pedro, who supports his family and ministry through construction work as a mason. He takes every job available. He travels from his rural community, Seven Miles, to San Ignacio, which has more job opportunities. After work each evening, he leads worship in his church. Last year, Pastor Pedro drove three hours one way, twice a week, to Santa Cruz village, where he helped plant a church and finish constructing their building in partnership with congregations in the United States. As part of his duties, he also supervises two pastors in two other rural villages.

Three days a week, Pastor Nelson travels two hours to reach his little farm. There he grows black beans, corn, and soy beans by hand. Twice a year, at the end of a grueling manual harvesting time, he takes his products to sell at market in San Ignacio with no promises of finding a buyer. He trusts the Lord. His pastoral commitments include supervising two churches and their leadership. Pastor Nelson also travels every evening, Monday through Sunday, to preach in a church in Belmopan, an hour away. His wife and four children go with him. It is their family time.

Elizabeth and Alfonso Ayala

These pastors and others—Sister Nieves, Brother Francisco, Brother Fidel, and more—take their call very seriously. With little or no pastoral training or support, they invest their lives serving God's people and reaching others for Christ. With devotion, zeal, and passion for God, these brothers and sisters constantly inspire and challenge us to be better servants and better partners in the mission to glorify God and edify his church.

—Alfonso Ayala
San Ignacio, Belize

ECUADOR

We'd noticed several new young men attending the Zabala church. All were in their late teens and early twenties. Their love for God was obvious, but because we travel to all the congregations in Ecuador, we're not always current with the lives of all believers in any given congregation.

Later, on another visit to Zabala, three of these "new" young men were leading worship. One in particular, Luis Miguel Erazo, was the lead singer and had a beautiful voice. It was a little untrained, but there was great potential and his spirit touched our hearts. We asked Pastor Marta about the influx of new faces to the church, and especially Luis. Marta beamed and responded, "Don't you remember Luis?"

Truthfully, we couldn't remember ever seeing him until several months ago. To our surprise, Marta told us that Luis and the others were once Sunday school children from the community. In fact, Luis had attended for several years. But as he entered his teenage years, he (like so many others) dropped out of church to enjoy life on his own terms.

Zabala Church, Ecuador

Unfortunately, Luis had fallen into drugs and drunkenness. These escalated to stealing in order to support the drugs. But one day, Marta related, Luis had stopped by the church, remembering that the church was the only place he'd ever known real peace.Even as a child, he realized that he'd found the presence of God there. So when the world had broken his heart, shattered his dreams, and destroyed his ability to feel, Luis headed home. When he did, like the prodigal son, he found open arms to welcome him.

As we labored through seminary classes last August, I watched the Zabala students with special delight. There, every day with a smile, sat Luis Miguel Erazo. His beautiful voice always sings praises to the heavenly Father who welcomed him home.

So many in this world—and sadly, at times, even in the church—think that social programs, tougher laws, more police, or a war on drugs will change the world and save our children. When will people realize that what they need is Jesus? He has always been the only answer and he still is.

—Jon Lambert
Quito, Ecuador

GUAM

Two stories remind us never to give up on people because God is at work, even if we aren't aware of it.

In December 2008 at a ballet Christmas concert, we were pleasantly surprised to meet a Japanese woman with whom Gary had worked closely while performing Japanese weddings over five years earlier. At that time, he'd talked many times with Hiroko about spiritual matters. Although her heart was open, there were obstacles to her coming to faith because of her busyness and respect for her Buddhist mother. But God works in amazing ways.

Some time later, Hiroko's daughter Raina was led to Christ by the mother of one of her ballet students. Raina changed so wonderfully that Hiroko was intrigued and started attending church with her. Eventually Hiroko also gave her life to Christ. The reason we were blessed to hear this good news is because of our new friendship with the family who has been discipling Hiroko and our attendance at their children's concert. Imagine Gary's joy as Hiroko thanked him for the seeds he sowed in her heart years ago that are now bearing fruit.

Then shortly after Christmas, the phone rang. The caller wanted to thank Gary for "saving my life" at a difficult time. "I'm sorry, he's not in," I responded, "but I'll be happy to give him your number, and may I tell him who is calling?" The man left his number but not his name, saying he wanted to surprise Gary. Curious, Gary returned the call and was reconnected with Mike.

The Bistritan family: Gwen, Gary, Randa, Jared, and Kelty

The story of their initial meeting is interesting. About 10 minutes from our house, down one of Guam's back roads, is another side road. It is somewhat secluded, near a place called Marbo Caves. Gary used to go there regularly to jog, but one day he found himself being chased by a man with a machete. Mentally prepared to defend himself, Gary was happy when they struck up a conversation instead. Mike was going through a hard time and was living in the jungle with not much more than the clothes on his back. (The property was owned by his extended family.) But when Gary stopped running there, he and Mike lost touch. Who would have guessed Mike would contact Gary so many years later? Shortly afterwards, Mike began attending our church.

We must always remember, "Let us not become weary in doing good, for at the proper time we will reap a harvest if we do not give up" (Galatians 6:9).

—Gwen Bistritan
Barrigada, Guam

JAPAN

Zonia Mitchell, long-time servant in Japan

In 2009, Japan celebrated the one hundred fiftieth anniversary of Protestant missions. Just two years before the Civil War broke out in America, the first Protestant missionaries arrived in the cities of Yokohama and Nagasaki.

One missionary teacher among them was a man named Guido Verbeck. Just 29 years old, he came with his new wife Maria, who was only 19. The Japan the Verbecks encountered had just "reopened" to the world after nearly 300 years of isolation. A strict ban against Christianity was still in effect when they arrived, and this wouldn't be lifted until 1873, 14 years later.

How would you "be a missionary" in that situation? Amazingly, Verbeck baptized one of the first Protestant Christians in his home as early as 1866. Equally astonishing is what that new believer, Murata Wakasa, did after his secret baptism in Nagasaki. Murata returned to Saga, his hometown (where I live), and reported his newfound faith in Christ to Lord Nabeshima, the ruler who had the power to end Murata's life upon hearing such a confession. Instead of executing Murata, Lord Nabeshima allowed his 51-year-old fellow government leader to freely practice his faith for the rest of his life. Today, Murata Wakasa's descendents are Christian, actively living out their joy-filled faith in Yokohama.

While many Japanese believers thank God for the lives and legacy of Verbeck and Murata, I'm thanking the Lord for the heritage of faith passed on to me by my Mitchell-Grantland grandparents, parents, and friends in the family of God. I'm also grateful for God's provision and blessing during the 20 years I've been a special assignment missionary in Japan with Church of God Global Missions. Thank you for your prayerful support of the continuing work of spreading the good news of Jesus in Japan, the Asia–Pacific region, and throughout the world.

—Zonia Mitchell
Saga, Japan

LATIN AMERICA

Adrian and Isidra Garcia were en route to a pastor's conference in Guatemala City when four armed men held up their bus. Passengers wept as they emptied their pockets into the bandits' satchel, pleading with the thieves to let them keep just enough money to buy return bus fares. Nothing doing. The Garcias lost 800 quetzales (U.S. $106) and arrived in the city penniless.

Unfortunately, this kind of thing happens often in Latin America. When their fellow pastors at the conference learned of the robbery, they raised an offering for the Garcias. Fortunately, this kind of thing happens often within the family of God in Latin America.

We learned much through training events we led this past year in Colombia, Peru, Panama, and elsewhere. We now know, for example, that nine of ten pastors, evangelists, worship leaders, and youth ministers who attend our International Forums for Kingdom Workers support their families with secular jobs. The Church of God has doctors, teachers, accountants, cab drivers, nurses, construction workers, salespersons, and other dual vocation professionals preaching the gospel. Most of them feel their educational experience adequately prepared them to lead churches, but they want to sharpen their knowledge of Scripture and develop their spiritual gifts. That's why we organize these forums and why folks like the Garcias come to them, despite the risks. Over the year, 105 church leaders from 11 countries participated in Kingdom Worker Forums.

David and Barbara Miller

We think the forums could also help reduce the crime rate. For example, Jenni is a relatively new Christian who joined the forum in Chepén, Peru. She had recently completed her teaching degree and was planning to accept one of several job offers in her hometown. But God had other plans. Jenni heard him calling her to teach in Tumbes, a city near the border with Ecuador. There she became involved in prison evangelism. Her pastor, Nicolas Perez, told us later that, although she'd never had any experience in jails before, Jenni believes God placed her in Tumbes to share Jesus with inmates.

Perhaps some of those thieves who rob bus passengers at gunpoint will one day hear about repentance and forgiveness and submit to the lordship of Christ. Not only would their lives change for the better, but travel might become less of a risk for the Garcías and other members of the family of God

—David Miller
Cochabamba, Bolivia

LEBANON

Camille and Hoda Melki

Farah, her husband, and their two daughters fled war in Iraq and came to Lebanon, where her husband eventually found a job illegally as a porter. Their house was poorly furnished, especially for winter, but they put mattresses on the floor to provide for seating for those of us from the Heart for Lebanon staff.

After welcoming us as we were distributing blankets, a part of our Iraqi Winterization Project, Farah was open to share both her story and fears with us. She was concerned about their daughters because of their restless and aggressive behavior that had developed after their arrival in Lebanon. She feared it might be the result of the many difficult experiences they'd endured, especially because she'd begun to notice how the children startled every time they heard loud noises that reminded them of the bombings in Iraq. We could see how their circumstances had taken a toll on the family as they shared their discouragement and anxiety in such a trying situation.

But Farah also testified to us about how she and her family had received Jesus as their personal Savior while they were yet in Iraq. As a result, Heart for Lebanon staff had the privilege of praying with them both during that first and subsequent home visits, providing encouragement and support. During those later visits, Farah told us enthusiastically about the local church the family had begun attending, a church recommended to them by our staff. The family has been greatly consoled as a result of this new church relationship.

Looking back to their journey from Iraq to Lebanon, Farah remembers how God was with them every step of the way. When she was leaving Iraq, she'd discovered that her legal papers had expired; she was afraid she would face further hardship as a result. Yet she prayed to God all the way for his protection and provision, and now she witnesses to answered prayers. This family joyfully celebrated New Year's Eve 2009 with their newfound church family in Lebanon.

And we are joyful as well that God can show his love through us.

—Camille Melki
Beirut, Lebanon

PARAGUAY

We had just sat down for lunch after an extremely hectic morning when we got the call. Someone from our church had died in a car accident and we were needed. Sigh. We had just been talking about how we needed a few hours to unwind from all our activities and get some sleep. That wouldn't happen this afternoon.

We gathered together songs for the funeral service and hastily made our way out the door. It was raining hard and the sky was dark, almost perfect conditions for the moment. Where we live, viewings are held in people's homes since there are no funeral parlors. We moved through the crowd of people that had come to pay their respects; at least 30 people had crammed into the small living room. I could feel myself starting to suffocate, not only because of my tight space, but because of the stench. Almost no one embalms bodies here because of the expense. Bodies must be buried as soon as possible to avoid odors. But sometimes relatives have to travel great distances to arrive and the body waits.

We were asked to lead the music, and Norberto began to strum, "What a Friend We Have in Jesus." As the people mourned and wailed loudly around us, I looked up at the sky-blue painted walls and asked God to open hearts as our pastor shared. We only had four songs on our sheet, and with one great hymn of the faith we seemed to be inventing a new melody with every verse!

As we were singing our unrehearsed hymns, Timmy fell asleep in my arms. He had no idea of the turmoil and ache of those around him. He was at peace with God and the world. Somehow, he became the center of attention, and everyone in the room had their eyes fixed on the innocent face of this sleeping boy next to the casket. Peace. Perfect peace.

The Kurrle family

Yes, Father, you give peace in the midst of pain, I thought to myself. And then the words of John 14:27 came into my mind: "Peace I leave with you; my peace I give you. I do not give to you as the world gives. Do not let your hearts be troubled and do not be afraid." Indeed, we experienced the peace of God's presence in that place and prayed that others would know him too.

—Julie Kurrle
Obligado, Itapua, Paraguay

SINGAPORE

Static is a killer in radio. No matter how good a program is, no one will listen if there is background static. You can't ignore it. It makes you irritable and robs you of peace until you turn it off.

We all have static in our lives as well—stuff going on in the background that people don't see, things we try to cope with on top of everyday life. Here is some static affecting members of our team: children in crisis, parents' failing health, a brother hospitalized, two fathers with cancer, a death in the family, a staff member with MS, one diagnosed with melanoma. The list could go on.

These types of things are not unique to missionaries. Everyone could make a list just as sobering. When these things happen, the world keeps spinning, but the static gets louder. It can get so loud that it starts to spill out into our everyday lives and begins to affect our relationships at home

The Ingram family

and work, and even with God. It can get so loud that we have a hard time hearing God at all. Static causes us to lose "the signal" and we can end up wondering if God really cares about what's going on in our lives.

At the same time, there is something wondrous about listening to a crystal clear broadcast. The announcer can sound as if he or she is talking just to you, sitting in the car or across the table. At HCJB Global (Asia Pacific), we work very hard at clarity, both in the signal and the message.

Sometimes in life we get moments of clarity—times we are sure of the way forward and of God's leading. Our team in India is experiencing one of those times. They recently began broadcasting a half-hour program from government radio stations in 14 different states. The weekly program can be heard by 65 percent of the country, or 650 million people. It's an amazing opportunity for our small team there.

I think that when Paul wrote in Romans that we should rejoice with those who rejoice and weep with those who weep, it was because he understood static and clarity. He understood that each of us will experience times when circumstances overwhelm us and cause us to question. He also understood that unshared success is desperately lonely.

Paul realized that we would need each other both in static and in clarity. So please weep and rejoice with us. Pray for our families who are experiencing a variety of deep personal struggles, and praise God for the exciting things he is doing through radio and other ministries in this region.

—Jeff Ingram
Singapore

UGANDA

In early March, we received a phone call from our district overseer, Stephen Kutosi, in eastern Uganda. That district is situated on the slopes of Mount Elgon, bordering Kenya. He told us that our church near Bududa

Digging out landslide victims

town had just experienced tragedy. On Sunday morning, February 28, as they were meeting for worship, a landslide carried the church building down the mountainside. Many other homes and buildings slid away at the same time. Due to the heavy rains (a seven-hour downpour) and deforestation of the mountain, the massive landslide swept through three villages, devastating everything in its path.

Initial information was that five members of the congregation died that morning, including the pastor (one of our few lady pastors), as well as many people in the community. But due to the thick mud and debris, many victims still had not been located, and it seemed the number of casualties would rise as hundreds were feared swallowed up by the destructive landslide. People in the area were literally digging survivors out of the debris by hand!

Please pray for this area as it struggles with the coldness, mud-logged houses, and the demoralizing effect of the tragedy on the community. The government of Uganda has declared many dead (and are providing over 100 coffins) and many missing due to this enormous calamity. More rains were expected as Uganda entered its rainy season. Please pray for our church family as they deal with loss of life and property. Pray also for their health and stamina while they continue looking for survivors and begin the recovery process. We are grateful that the national Church of God in Uganda was able to respond immediately by sending representatives into the area to assist with blankets, household items, and food relief.

It seems there are many natural disasters happening in the world these days. Life is so precarious, but one thing we know with certainty: when we have Christ, we have hope and a future no matter what the circumstance. As a church family, let us keep each other in prayer!

—Tim and Colleen Stevenson
Kampala, Uganda

Behind the Scenes

THE PRODIGAL DAUGHTER (page 6) Africa has been Kay Critser's home since 1969 when she went as a single missionary to Kenya. After marrying in 1978, she and Sherman have served in Tanzania, Congo, Uganda, and Côte d'Ivoire. Most recently, Kay helped the young Ivorian church begin outreach into neighboring Burkina Faso, where 75 percent of the people follow Islam or traditional religions. The initial outreach was in February 2009 when five Ivorian church leaders and four missionaries visited. After 10 days, 38 people had accepted Christ, including Adeline, of this story. Plans call for a permanent ministry couple to go there in 2010.

The fledgling church in Burkina Faso

ANOTHER DAY IN PARADISE, **THE SCAR**, and **THE FINGERPRINTS OF GOD** (pages 9, 76)—Canadians Tim and Colleen Stevenson served as special assignment missionaries in Uganda from 1986 to 1989. They returned as career missionaries in 1990 and have been there ever since. Their varied assignments find them relating to several central African nations, as well as to three Church of God missionary boards—in Canada, the United States, and Germany. Colleen is the daughter of longtime missionaries to Africa, Stanley and Marion Hoffman.

Tim and Colleen Stevenson

WITH MY OWN EYES (page 12)—The Church of God was launched in Zambia in 1986. After serving in East Africa for 27 years, missionaries Stanley and Marion Hoffman relocated to Zambia in 1993 to work hand-in-hand with national leader Afeck Lungu, who traveled with them to the village where Mailesi Ndao and her family met and accepted Jesus Christ. Today Mailesi is national leader of the Church of God that numbers some 400 congregations and more than 45,000 constituents.

Mailesi Ndao

AN UNLIKELY SERVANT (page 15)—Missionary Kay Critser translated this originally French story by one of her theological education by extension (TEE) students. After finishing the six-year TEE program in December 2008, Kaume Yao was trained to lead his own TEE groups, currently two, one in the city and one in a village. He has also been appointed as an advisor to the executive council of the national church. About him, Kay says, "We believe this young man has much potential in ministry here in Côte d'Ivoire. It's been my honor to watch him grow these past seven years."

Yao Kaumé making bricks

FOUR EGGS OF GRATITUDE (page 17)—After serving as a medical missionary in Uganda since 2004, Glenna Phippen returned to her native Canada in December 2009. She is grateful that the facilities of all four clinics operated by the Church of God were both upgraded and updated during her tenure, thanks to diligent efforts of faithful supporters and work campers. After six months of itinerating, Glenna will settle in Edmonton in July 2010, work part time in nursing, and seek ministry opportunities in her home city and church, First Church of God, Edmonton.

Glenna Phippen holding her namesake

A MIRACLE NAMED RHEA (page 20)—On May 8, 2009, Doug and Danette Beisley wrote this e-mail: "After 108 days in the hospital, baby Rhea was able to go home this afternoon. Rhea is about eight pounds now and totally breast feeding. Mother's Day is this Sunday. What a gift to Rochelle." The Beisleys have been missionaries in New Zealand since 2004. Rochelle and Steve Boyle are the parents of two sons, ages 10 and 2, and Rhea (Ray-uh).

Baby Rhea and family

SIT STILL, MY DAUGHTER (page 24)—Cheryl and Bernie Barton have been missionaries in Japan for 31 years. Cheryl was first diagnosed with renal cell carcinoma in March 2009 and underwent successful kidney removal in Japan in April. When the cancer returned in September and was inoperable, Cheryl began drug therapy that they believe will be effective in chasing the cancer into remission so that they can continue their long ministry in Japan. Granddaughter Hosanna was born December 29, 2009, in Tokyo.

Cheryl Barton and Hosanna

BUS JOURNEY TO HOPE (page 27)—Leaderwell Pohsngap is international director of Global LEAD (leadership equipping and development) Alliance. Facilitating leadership development in local churches around the world, the alliance offers training seminars worldwide—one of the reasons Leaderwell travels so frequently

Leaderwell (right) in Colombia

from his home in northeast India. His experience in developing leaders began in the 1980s when he and his wife, Rivulet, taught at what is now Kima International School of Theology (KIST) in Kenya.

DISASTER IN THE PHILIPPINES (page 29)—Linda Mason, associate director of Children of Promise, shared this story after her trip to the Philippines to assess the needs of sponsored children in the aftermath of devastating Typhoon Ketsana. By early March 2010, Children of Promise sponsors had given more than $57,000 to help the families of Filipino sponsored children repair and/or rebuild their homes. Children of Promise sponsors over 3,800 children in 23 nations, including India, Thailand, Russia, Egypt, Haiti, Jamaica, Ecuador, Colombia, Nicaragua, Ghana, and Tanzania.

children of promise
sponsor a child change a life...

AND GOD IS IN IT (page 32)—Jodie Ackerman wrote this story in the days immediately following the Haiti earthquake on January 12, 2010. After the earthquake, she began helping first grade and younger children at the international school where she's taught since 1997 while her husband, John, continued to assist Heartline trauma and medical clinic. On March 4, he was able to resume his regular clinics at Prospere, minus his nurse Eden, who was still helping her hospitalized daughter recover from quake-related injuries. (Sadly, Eden lost her son and a sister in the quake.) John was also working closely with an assessment team in planning where Church of God efforts should go for long-term help and rebuilding.

Resilient Haitian refugee children

TALE OF THE TOOTHPASTE BOX CASKETS (page 36)—Dave Gosse, Christian education director of the Church of God in Jamaica, requested this story from Sheldon Anderson, one of the 75-plus students who have graduated in the 25-year-history of the Leadership Training Institute. Its three-year program is built around modules, with each module being conducted over five consecutive weekends. As Dave explains, the institute was established "not just to provide a cadre of pastors...but also to harness and develop church members...to become change agents in both the church and the wider society."

Sheldon Anderson and family

THE ACUITY LEVEL PRINCIPLE (page 38)—Missionaries since 1986 in the Caribbean island nation of Haiti, John and Jodie Ackerman carry out their ministries in different settings. John conducts two weekly medical clinics in rural Prospere—conducted in the basement of the Prospere Church of God. Jodie is a kindergarten teacher in an international school in Port-au-Prince, Haiti's capital city. They are the parents of two daughters, one a high school student still at home.

Jessica, Jodie, and John Ackerman

WADING WITH GOD (page 40)—While some think a missionary's life as exciting and glamorous, each of the 65 special assignment, missionary apprentice, or career missionaries on the field as of December 2009 know the truth firsthand. Sometimes cultures clash, expectations exceed funding or time, children get sick (as do aging parents at home), and a host of other challenges conspire to wrest a missionary's peace and threaten to cause the certainty of calling to dim. Please pray for the Church of God missionary staff in all five regions of the world.

HOLY WASHING (page 42)—The author of this story is a Church of God individual working in Eurasia who chooses to write anonymously in order to protect believers, contacts, and the work he is doing in a nation where Christians are persecuted. He asks for readers to join in a prayer campaign called P50K ("Pray for 50,000" new believers in this country) and to believe that the Lord will bring a great harvest, even in this difficult land.

Courtyard scene in the country of "holy washing"

IN THE PALM OF HIS HAND (page 45)—Andrei Kolegov has served as associate pastor of the Church of God in Chelyabinsk, Russia, since 1995. One of four Churches of God in Russia, his congregation has grown into a vibrant church through the leadership of national pastors and an active lay-leadership team involved in such things as prison and orphanage outreach. A gifted communicator who is passionate about sharing the gospel, Andrei has translated many Christian materials from English into Russian, including books by Max Lucado, discipleship resources, and Church of God resources.

Andrei Kolegov

YOU DON'T HAVE TO BE AN EAGLE TO SOAR (page 47)—Kathy and David Simpson are second career missionaries. Kathy had spent 25 years in social work, with David working in human resources management in Warsaw, Indiana, when God called them to become missionaries. Resigning their positions and leaving

Kathy and David Simpson

their two adult sons behind, they relocated to Bulgaria in 2005. Among their joys is watching Bulgarian Christians move from being observers to becoming full participants in their faith.

CHOCOLATE JESUS (page 51)—During 17 years as missionaries, Rhonda and Kelley Philips helped pioneer the church in Chelyabinsk, Russia. Following this, they served as regional coordinators for Europe and the Middle East while living in Hungary and Germany. Now they are part of an international team of seven people committed to Gateway Berlin, the first phase of a strategic gateway approach to ministry in major urban centers around the world. They are the parents of three adult children and one yet at home.

CINDERELLA'S DELIGHT (page 54)—It's often a juggling act for a missionary mother to manage all her responsibilities. For Kara Goldman, this means being available for Manning (12), Brennan (9), and Abigail (7), in addition to husband Dwayne, serving the church in Chelyabinsk, Russia, and being a graduate student. And due to changes in visa regulations, the Goldmans have had to exit Russia and renew visas every 90 days since 2008, making it very hard to settle and slow down. But God continues to teach them how to be still in the midst of it all.

The Goldman family

BIRD'S EYE VIEW and **THE FINGERPRINTS OF GOD** (pages 56, 76)—Regional coordinators for Latin America since 2005, David and Barbara Miller are especially grateful for two Church of God Ministries programs that assist international missions work. Among other things, Project Link supports several projects in Latin America that specifically promote discipleship and leader development. Spread the Word (STW) encourages

The Millers

young people to fund projects promoting evangelism overseas. For further information, contact Church of God Ministries (800-848-2464).

TWO GIRLS, TWO COUNTRIES (page 61)—After 17 years as missionaries in Costa Rica, Kathi and Wayne Sellers returned to the United States in 2008. Kathi now serves as recruitment and personnel administrator for Global Missions. She shares that 18-year-old Xochilt continues to be very busy at church—in the Sunday school program, as worship leader at the Tuesday night church service, as a helper with the youth group, and as leader of the church's worship dance team. She also is studying physical therapy at university.

Kathi and Wayne Sellers

IN A BESIEGED CITY (page 64)—The year 2009 was significant in Abby Smith's life. Not only did she graduate in May from Anderson University School of Theology, but she was also commissioned in June as a special assignment missionary to Colombia. Later that fall, she rejoiced at the news that she had raised sufficient funds to leave for Costa Rica in January, where she would enroll in a three-month advanced Spanish-language class. Following graduation, she relocated to Colombia in April 2010.

Abby Smith

OUTBREAK IN OFELIA and **THE FINGERPRINTS OF GOD** (pages 67, 76)—Jon and Karen Lambert are grateful for the 13 years they've partnered as missionaries with the Church of God in Ecuador. But they are also thankful for their two adult children and for the December

Pastor Milton and Lilly of Ophelia Church

23, 2009, birth of Elena Noel Engelbrecht, their first grandchild. They also are grateful for the faithfulness of God's family with prayer and financial support that helps to make their ministry possible.

LAST WORD, FIRST WORD and **THE FINGERPRINTS OF GOD** (pages 70, 76)—As a part of her missionary assignment in Paraguay, Julie Kurrle serves as national director of the Children of Promise program in that South American nation where she and her husband, Norberto, have served as special assignment missionaries since 2002. Their son Timmy, whose peaceful expression as he slept at a funeral reminded Julie of the peace of Christ, was born in Paraguay in 2005.

Julie, Timmy, and Norberto Kurrle

THE FINGERPRINTS OF GOD

- **Kirk Bookout** is donor relations consultant for the World Ministry Advance team of Church of God Ministries, Anderson, Indiana. (page 77)
- **Alfonso Ayala** and his wife Elizabeth have served as missionaries since 1987 in Central America, first in Honduras (1987–88) and since 1989 in Belize. (page 78)
- Canadians **Gwen and Gary Bistritan** have been missionaries on Guam since 1985. They have pastored the two congregations there and currently are involved in helping the Church of God reach out into other neighboring islands. (page 80)
- **Zonia Mitchell** has been serving in Japan as a special assignment missionary since 1989. She teaches English at Saga University and is a lay servant at Saga Church of God. (page 81)
- **Camille Melki** is director of Heart for Lebanon, a Christian relief organization serving refugees and displaced people in Lebanon. (page 83)